Uprooting Economics

A Manifesto for Change

Bart Nooteboom

Professor Emeritus, Tilburg University,
the Netherlands

 Edward Elgar
PUBLISHING

Cheltenham, UK • Northampton, MA, USA

Published by
Edward Elgar Publishing Limited
The Lypiatts
15 Lansdown Road
Cheltenham
Glos GL50 2JA
UK

Edward Elgar Publishing, Inc.
William Pratt House
9 Dewey Court
Northampton
Massachusetts 01060
USA

A catalogue record for this book
is available from the British Library

Library of Congress Control Number: 2019951084

This book is available electronically in the **Elgar**online
Economics subject collection
DOI 10.4337/9781789908428

ISBN 978 1 78990 841 1 (cased)
ISBN 978 1 78990 843 5 (paperback)
ISBN 978 1 78990 842 8 (eBook)

Typeset by Servis Filmsetting Ltd, Stockport, Cheshire
Printed and bound by CPI Group (UK) Ltd, Croydon, CR0 4YY

Contents

Introduction

This book is radical in its criticism of fundamental assumptions and proposals for a new economics. That is needed in view of the present political upheaval, such as the emergence of populism and re-emergence of nationalism and authoritarian regimes. This is due, in part, to economic effects and ideas in economics that are considered to be unjust and inhumane. Of course, the present book is not the first one that is critical of economics, and I build on previous such books (Kay, 2003; Cassidy, 2009; Sandel, 2012; Skidelsky and Skidelsky, 2012). The present book takes a more interdisciplinary approach, with insights from economics, sociology, cognitive science, social psychology and philosophy. Economics is needed for basic notions of markets, competition, scarcity and efficiency. Sociology is needed to account for the social constitution of people. Cognitive science is needed to deal with knowledge and learning, how ideas develop and uncertainty. Social psychology is needed to deal with limited rationality and the role of decision heuristics. Philosophy is needed for ethics and the human relations of 'self and other'. I build on a life of research in these fields (in economics, innovation, organization, collaboration, trust and philosophy).

The resulting new economics is no longer about autonomous individuals but about people involved with each other, developing through interactions between them. That is the central theme of the book, where its coherence lies. It is a relational economics: less contract, hierarchy and control, and more trust and mutual adjustment; with markets, but not where they become immoral, and with more correction of their failures; competition, but also collaboration; not only instrumental value to achieve prosperity, but also intrinsic value – value in itself, of things, work and relations; not aimed at immunity to each other, autonomy and independence, but at community and commonality; less vertical and hierarchical, with more horizontal control, in mutual influence.

Some contract and control are often needed, to reduce risk in relations, but the price one pays for that is loss of intrinsic value of room in the relationship for initiative and mutual adjustment. There is more intrinsic value in acting on trust, and for that one may be willing to surrender some profit and accept some more risk. More room for trust yields more risk but also more perspective for initiative, improvization and self-direction, taking one's own responsibility.

In the economy and in conduct there is much uncertainty: one does not always know what can happen, what possibilities can present themselves, and what preferences one will have. That uncertainty is commercial, technological, political and relational. Uncertainty is more pervasive especially in innovation. Economics is geared to deal with risk, where one does not know what will happen but does know what can happen, so that one can calculate probabilities. It is not geared to deal with uncertainty, where one does not even know what can happen, which often emerges only after choice and action. Keynes was one of the few economists who took uncertainty seriously, and this has been picked up in post-Keynesian economics (Skidelsky, 2009). Inability to deal with uncertainty implies an inability to deal adequately with especially radical innovation (which was my field of work in economics).

The future is often incalculable. Under uncertainty, control of relationships is a problem because one does not know what can happen, and hence what one should lay down in a contract. That soon becomes a straitjacket that blocks requisite change. Hierarchy falters because one works with others, or employs them, because they know or can do things you can't, and then how can you tell them what to do? That requires less control and more trust.

More than ever, due to uncertainty, and the complexity and speed of change one cannot do things alone, and one needs contributions from others, in collaboration. Less 'intelligent design', planning and organization in mergers and acquisitions is needed, and more adaptation, with trials and errors, in alliances. With the surprise they offer, the most valuable relationships are the most uncertain.

Up to a point, trust can be reasoned about, but beyond that point it is a leap in the dark. That requires the virtue of courage. According to old economic thought trust cannot survive in markets, because it requires sacrifice without adequate returns, and under the pressure of competition in markets one cannot afford that. So much the worse for those markets. In many cases competition is so imperfect as to allow some leeway for give and take. Markets change, and survival under that change brings uncertainty, and if one does not accept that in the leap of faith, then one is certain not to survive that change. Without trust there is no dealing with uncertainty.

All this, I will argue, requires a replacement of the old, still prevailing, utility ethics, in neoliberalism and economics, that only looks at outcomes in the form of the highest utility for the largest number of people, and not at the quality of intentions and the intrinsic value of processes that produce outcomes. A shift is needed to an ethics of the classical virtues of prudence, courage, moderation and justice. Prudence is needed for a balance between protection against uncertainty and its utilization, between a critical evaluation of trustworthiness and a leap of faith. It is also needed for being reasonable when something goes wrong, not to immediately accuse the other of cheating but to give the benefit of doubt and ask for an explanation. Courage is needed to dare to take the leap of faith of trust, and to engage in the openness which makes one vulnerable to criticism, but which is

needed for trust. Moderation is needed for joint
profit, in give and take, not to begrudge the other.
Justice requires sacrifices, also where the reward
for it cannot be calculated. The motivation for this
comes from inside, not because it is obligatory but
because that is how one sees oneself, because one
wants those virtues. They have intrinsic value.

The book is aimed at a wide but intellectual audience, in academia and outside it: policymakers,
politicians, civil servants, business leaders, profes-
sionals, consultants and citizens generally, who
are interested in a wide perspective on current
society and economy. Many people in society are
concerned about the economy and economics, and
those concerns need to be addressed.

The orientation of the book towards a wide
audience and multiple disciplines has consequences for its presentation. I do not assume
much knowledge of the disciplines involved,
explain what I use, and employ much illustration
from practice. I employ insights from different
streams in economics, and from sociology, social
psychology, cognitive science and philosophy, in
particular ethics, and a number of my views are
personal. That is broad, too broad some may say,
but I try to put the pieces together in a coherent
fashion. The presentation is scholarly in that I use
arguments, not just opinions, as much as possible,
and employ insights from science and their connections. I refer to a number of authors crucial
to this book without striving for completeness
that would overwhelm non-specialist readers. I

show where ideas come from and what I make up myself. This is in part the usual ethic of not stealing ideas from others, but oriented not so much at justifying myself to scientific colleagues as at indicating connections for readers who want to pursue them.

1. Crisis of capitalism

A reform, or revolution even, is needed of the
economy as a system and economics as a discipline. That is not a luxury but a political emer-
gency. The need for it is evident from present
clashes between economics and society. This
chapter offers an elaboration of that need: the
symptoms. Then follows the diagnosis: what is
going wrong, and the need for therapy: a new economics. Next, an elaboration of how the economy
really works, in different industries. And then, the
therapy: a proposal for a new economics, in fact
present economics stood on its head.

Economic value

I am not going to claim that economics is entirely
wrong, and I continue to use elements from
it. Society has much to be grateful for in the
economy, in prosperity and employment. Markets
are indispensable for that. If it works well, it goes
as follows.

Businesses borrow money to invest in knowledge, tools, machines, materials and competence,
to develop and produce products that society
needs. They make a profit, from which they repay
the loans and further invest, and thus create

employment and growth. In practice it often does work like that, but increasingly it does not.

The demand for products is inflated with advertising, with an appeal to greed and insatiability. Production and distribution cause environmental damage that is not included in the price of products. Profits are not always spent on production and development, but are regularly used to buy other firms to achieve profit growth, without improving those firms or products. Thus, a 'hedge fund' buys a firm with borrowed money, imposes a fee, takes the firm off the stock market, pays the loan and fee from selling part of the firm, firing staff, or economizing on wages or benefits, or on research and development. This increases the short-term profitability of the firm, which raises its share value, and then the firm is sold again on the market. The argument to defend this is that in this way firms are penalized for not fully utilizing their profit potential. But it goes at the expense of the long-term potential of the firm, banking on the market's myopia for the short term, profit in the next quarter.

Sometimes there is a lack of market dynamics, but increasingly also an excess. The market is not to be set aside, but to be set right. Economic thought has its value, up to a point, but has encroached too far beyond the economy, in an ideology that is corroding society. I do not want to abolish economics but to stand it on its head, in a different approach that on crucial points is its opposite.

Political costs

Often, what runs aground in society is not a matter of evil intent but of a way of thinking that had good reasoning but lost its bearings, became myopic, and has congealed in perverse systems of thought and action from which it cannot disentangle itself. The thinking becomes an ideology, of which one cannot see, or cannot admit, that it is an ideology. And it needs that blindness for it to work.

This yields what I call 'system tragedy'. The advocates are so entangled in the system that they simply do not see what is wrong with it, but are willing to explain it to the opponents one more time. And if that does not clinch it, the opposition is in a plight of the dumb. The protagonists and profiteers of the system then are aggrieved that one is not grateful to them and does not hold them in esteem. Others, taken up in the system, get entangled in roles and positions with which they disagree but which they cannot afford to refuse, for fear of loss of position, recognition or income – until the bomb bursts.

In present economic thought concerning society, the myopia is that one sees only the economic costs and revenues of the conduct of firms. One gives insufficient regard to the political costs of pollution and dodging its regulation, the lobbies of large firms, excessive salaries and bonuses, subsidies on location and on energy, and tax dodges, and all that under the threat to move employment abroad if they do not get their way. A substantial part of politics apparently is blind to the political costs, or surrenders to the arm twisting involved.

The legitimacy of business lies in the satisfaction of needs in society; preservation of nature is such a need and if business does not satisfy it, it is renouncing its task.

Where are those political costs? They lie in the rise of populism, the uprising of the 'yellow vests', kindled by partly justified grudges over unequal rights and incomes, and the favours given to large firms and shareholders at the expense of the poor, erosion of expenditure on care and education, and of reward, security, quality, continuity and conditions for labour.

Socialists also have let themselves be seduced by the economic imperative of the 'supply side', i.e. business. 'It's the economy, stupid', was the motto, on the left and the right. One is getting worried by populism but continues to provoke it with economic and political indecencies. With their 'third way', Bill Clinton in the US, Tony Blair in the UK, Gerhard Schröder in Germany and Wim Kok in the Netherlands took a turn to the right, in surrender to globalization. To be fair, the negative effects this would have were not clear then. Now they are, and one can no longer close one's eyes to them. Here I use a definition of the left from Stephanie Mudge (2018): 'Representation of those who are otherwise not represented'. That concerned the poor and the excluded, and now also concerns refugees.

The problem is not only one of large multi-nationals, but also of other areas of misuse of power, as in professions that exert a monopoly of knowledge or a cartel to enforce excessive remuneration, such as medical specialists. There, one can say, there is not too much but too little market dynamics.

Populism

Populism demonstrates growing dissatisfaction of the people, and exploits that for electoral gain. Part of the grudge lies in the justified suspicion that the people carry the burden while especially large, multinational corporations are let off the hook. And, indeed, government goes easy on those out of fear that otherwise they will take their employment elsewhere. That is a genuine problem. In fact, national government is not up to matching the power of those companies, is not in a position to counter them on its own. There is a solution for that, in bundling powers of nations, in the EU, for example, but then populists are against that. They exploit the frustration but obstruct the solution.

However, next to economics there is much more at stake. Is populism a shout for individualism, the citizen at the centre, or the opposite, a call for restoration of community, the social? Such community, with values that are shared to some extent, yields a buffer against uncertainty, on which one can fall back in times of adversity.

Such opposition between individual and community is only imaginary, since the individual is rooted in the social, and that is precisely what economics has lost sight of, or never had in sight. And the social is rooted in the local. That is one of two reasons for the craving for nationalism: restoration of a sense of local roots.

One of the strongest bonds, arising from evolution, is that of kin. The more closely people are genetically related, the more sacrificing and altruistic they are, as with parents to their offspring, siblings, cousins, etc. The bonding strength of kin terminology, of 'brotherhood', 'family', 'blood', etc. may be adopted, hijacked, so to speak, in 'pseudo-kin', even when relations are hardly genetic. Examples abound: 'brotherhood' among soldiers, soccer fans, motor clubs, gangs. And in this way ethnic divisions creep in, where appearance, colour and culture are connected to kinship.

Another source of nationalistic prejudice, not arising from genetic commonality but often allied with 'pseudo-kin', lies in 'parochial altruism': the human being has a deep suspicion, probably anchored in genes shared universally, against outsiders, to be recognized in different appearance, religion and habits. That has been amply studied in social science. Next to a drive for self-interest and survival the human being has an instinctive drive for recognition and being valued in a community, and is even willing to make sacrifices for others for this.[1] That is the good news. The bad news is that this is accompanied by suspicion of and discrimination against outsiders. And that was needed, in evolution, to protect altruism within the group from exploitation by invading outsiders with different genes, who would otherwise get the upper hand, competing away the altruistic genes. That is what lies beneath the repulsion towards refugees.

The conclusion is not to give in to this prejudice but to better combat it, and make an effort to integrate outsiders so that they are felt to belong to one's own group. Nothing works better for that than to include them in joint activities, in a shared fate, in taking part in work and education. Then immigrants turn out to be human. Then they become colleagues.

People belong to different in-groups, in communities, jobs, professions, memberships, etc. and someone who 'belongs to them' in one context may 'belong to us' in another. This multiplicity is good news, since prejudice in one context may be side-tracked with commonality in another. Robert Sapolsky (2019) quotes an example: 'During WWII .... A British officer and his prisoner, a German officer, shifted categories of enmity into something resembling a friendship that lasted decades when they discovered by chance that they shared a love of Greek classics'.

Next to populism, is there no other resistance to excesses of capitalism? The 'Occupy Wall Street' movement protested, most of all, against the misconduct of banks, but it has since evaporated. The movement on purpose did not choose the parliamentary path of developing a political party. As a result it did not muster political power. Recently, there has been a rise, in France, with some spread to other countries, of the 'yellow vests', but that also appears to be dissipating due to a lack of leadership and focus.

What liberalism?

How was the connection between the individual and the social and the local lost? There, liberalism went off the track. It began well but lost its bearings. But what liberalism are we talking about?

'Liberalism' is an ambiguous notion. A leftist form of it recognizes the communal and social, a rightist form emphasizes the individual and its own responsibility. After World War II, there was a period when attempts were made to balance the two. But from the 1970s it took a right turn, in 'neoliberalism'.

One meaning of liberalism is also that of liberal, constitutional democracy. That does not only include free elections. Illiberal, autocratic regimes, such as those of Putin, Erdogan and Orban, claim those, though in practice in elections the opposition is hampered, in access to the media and preparation of the elections. In any case, elections do not suffice. It is also a matter of equality under the law, rights for minorities, freedoms of speech, association and religion, and separation of powers (of government, parliament and the judiciary). Authoritarian regimes dodge those.

Autocratic regimes flourish on seduction of the people by the charismatic leader who claims to listen to his/her people and to represent them directly and to be their embodiment, making parliament superfluous. The decisiveness of the leader stands in contrast to the bumbling of democracy, which can only arrive at delayed and watered-down decisions, that at the fall of government have to be redone all over again in a slightly different direction. Its strength lies precisely in that, since in the democratic process of oversight and journalistic investigation elites do not get the chance to buttress themselves as infallible and irreplaceable. The authoritarian leader can do that and deflect criticism onto some scapegoat, such as a criminalized opposition or foreign power, or apostate, or refugees.

A deeper background of democracy arises from the insight, in the philosophy of knowledge, that the notion of a single, univocal truth is problematic, an illusion, and mankind requires a variety of views, from different, contrasting perspectives.

Liberalism more widely arose in the late 1700s, and there had a leftist load, directed against the rule of nobility and monarchy, that erupted in the French Revolution. Later, in the late 1800s it obtained the meaning of social reform – in the US in the 'New Deal' of Franklin Roosevelt in the 1930s. That developed into the application of the ideas of Keynes, in the management of demand with public spending to maintain economic growth and employment. That went on until in the 1970s, with the occurrence of persistent 'stagflation': inflation combined with low growth and high unemployment. That was taken to contradict Keynesianism, though some pointed at shocks in the price of oil as the cause.

Then economic thought made a turn of 180 degrees. Not the Keynesian fiscal policy of government expenditure, but the monetary policy of managing the quantity of money, promoted by Milton Friedman, for the benefit of markets. Demand was no longer central, but the supply of firms in markets. Where in Keynesianism government manipulated the market, now the market manipulated government. Rising unemployment was no longer attributed to low government spending but to high wages. The turnaround was presented as liberation from a leftist ideology, to be replaced by the objective truth of the market, in 'shedding ideological feathers'. That is equally an ideology but one in denial of justice. To work, ideology must be presented as objective truth, here of markets. People do not let themselves be guided by a narrative that is admittedly an invention.

Attention turned primarily to international and financial markets, with a growing influence of financial institutions. Then, in the 1980s, neo-liberalism obtained a rightist connotation, becoming synonymous with 'libertarianism', the ideology of markets that only work in the absence of government 'meddling' in 'laissez faire'.

There is a 'neoliberalism index' that scores political programmes on four factors: own responsibility, labour as a market value, fewer protective social measures and a greater presence of professions than blue-collar labour, the poor and unemployed. That index increased notably among leftist parties; among rightist parties it was already high (Mudge, 2018, pp. 60, 61). In the ideas of the 'third way', of Clinton in the US, Blair in the UK, Schröder in Germany and Kok in the Netherlands, the left moved along in a turn to the right, partly from the perceived need to give an answer to the rise of Reagan in the US and Thatcher in the UK.

Later, markets will be discussed extensively. I will defend the paradoxical thesis that markets go too far as well as not far enough. The market is an important part of the problem but also of the solution. I will unravel where one lies and where the other, and how to deal with that.

Capitalism has not only derailed in an excess of markets, where they are not desirable, and from lobbies of large firms, but also because large firms themselves obstruct markets, in monopolies and oligopolies, or dodge the necessary oversight and regulation where markets are desirable.

Locality and flexibility

Back to the grounds for populism. The human being derives its identity from personal interaction, which flourishes best in local contact of some duration. Some time is required to get to know each other and build trust. In other words, the human being requires a sufficient degree of community, with a certain shared ethic. I do not want to idealize communities. The most violent derailments of intrigue, hatred, envy and feuds of revenge can arise there, precisely because people are tied together. There must be room for entry and exit, and contacts outside the community, for fresh ideas and to prevent rust and stickiness.

People used to find community in religious ties and social bonds of neighbourhood, school, sport, etc. and also in a job, in a firm, often in teams, and after work in the pub together. For many lower educated people both sorts of connections have disappeared. Communities were broken up by increase of scale, and concentration of work outside communities, departure of work to lower wage countries, and razing of building development for roads, offices and shopping malls, and now what remains is perceived to have priority for refugees. The higher educated and more mobile people found community in the larger firms or professional associations that remained.[2] But that also is crumbling in individualization of work and shorter periods of employment.

With arguments of economy of scale, Western multinationals enticed developing countries, in Africa, South America and Asia, to let the foreign corporations exploit their resources of land (agriculture), primary goods (oil, minerals, diamonds) and cheap labour (in clothing, electronics) and add value to them and generate profits not locally but in their own countries. Small-scale, labour-intensive local activities in farming and artisanship were seen as backward and inefficient, and in a narrow economic perspective they were, but they were viable in community-based collaboration, in sharing resources and activities (seeds, ploughing, harvesting, training) and thus distributing costs and risks. Those were pushed aside, and people flocked to cities where they supplied cheap labour under poor working conditions, to the profit of the multinationals.

The dominant stream of economic thought had no eye for all this. On the contrary: the central tenet was that of 'comparative advantage' and maximal flexibility: locally one should focus on where one was relatively resourceful, and other things were to be obtained in trade with others. Labour and capital should not be locally tied but maximally flexible, to move to where its revenue was highest. Comparative advantage was to the advantage of the developed countries, while at the time when they were not yet developed themselves they closed off their markets in order to get a chance to develop (Stiglitz, 2002).

Local roots are seen as rigid and that, the suggestion is, is always bad. That is the rhetoric of maximum flexibility. But often that is counterproductive, also from a purely economic perspective. That applies both for local roots and businesses as places. It is good for both business and workers to invest in knowledge, skills and relations that are specific, and have some continuity, for the firm. For the firm because it yields speciality products, with higher profit margins, and for workers because it lends more depth to the job. Such investments require some continuity of job and teams, otherwise those investments will not be made, and that yields loss of quality, next to the fact that some continuity of work is more pleasurable because it gives the opportunity for relations of collaboration. So, it should not be about maximum but about optimal flexibility: the sufficient duration of location without yielding rigidity.

Identity

In present society and public debate, identity plays an important role. In populism this means especially national identity: in Europe as Jewish-Christian, or based on the Enlightenment, or on a Romanticist sense of being a unique people. But people also seek identity in their place in society: as feminist, LGBT, scientist, or motor rider. What is the meaning of 'identity'?

There is *individual* identity ('who am I?') and *collective* identity ('who are we?'). There is also *categorial* identity ('where do I/we belong?') and *existential* identity ('how to we experience ourselves?'). For the individual, existential identity is *personal* identity. For the group it is *cultural* identity. Existential identity is connected with questions such as 'what do I/we want?', corresponding values, and the question 'how do I/

we think?'. Individual identity is connected with collective identity. One can hardly be part of a group that is at odds with who one is and what one thinks and does, and collective identity contributes to the formation of individual identity.

Individual identity is an intriguing notion. It suggests that in having that identity one is identical to oneself, remains the same with it. But the self is not constant, and not unambiguous. It is multiple and shifts in time, though it has a certain stability, if all is well. Where does that come from? From the body.[3]

Survival of the body requires sufficient coherence and stability of metabolic processes. Those processes yield mental representations in the brain which guide those processes. 'Representation' may not be the right term here. That suggests a mirror image, but intended here is the meaning of 'reproduction', a process of re-enactment rather than mirroring. There is interaction between the formation of those representations and action. Mental representations guide action and are formed in it. If in that process there was insufficient coherence and stability, the body could not survive.

Here I build on a philosophical tradition of pragmatism, with American roots (with the philosophers Peirce, James and Dewey), and connections or similarities among some European continental philosophers (Wittgenstein, in his later work, and Heidegger).

One develops a character and personality, along a path of life, as a totality of attitudes, response and conduct, in interaction with the physical and social environment. The individual literally stands or falls with coherence in the body. Without body there is no identity, and in death we lose it. In sum: in the body all impressions, movements and experiences come together. Those form dispositions, impulses and ideas on the basis of experience, and they are tied to the body, along a unique path of life.

If indeed the self is in ongoing development, then what is authenticity, truth to one's 'real' self? Where in time does that lie? How can one be true to something that is in development and furthermore one does not know perfectly? The idea of a self as something given beforehand that manifests itself invariantly is not only unrealistic but also, in my view, scary. Then one is condemned to an original self. Then authenticity perhaps is more that one commits oneself to utilize the opportunity to develop an identity, in the realization of potential and development of new potential, in interaction with one's environment.

In a recent book Francis Fukuyama (2018) claimed that personal identity is oriented towards recognition, to be noticed and appreciated, which he traced back to the ancient Greek notion of 'thymos', used, among others, by Plato. I see that differently. Thymos is the urge for action, to manifestation of the self in the world. That does not by definition require recognition. That would reduce all striving for excellence, in entrepreneurship, sports, science, health care, craftmanship, politics, etc. to a form of narcissism. It can also be about its intrinsic value, as giving meaning to life and developing and employing one's talents.

Thinking in boxes or relations

What is collective identity? The human being has a tenacious tendency to think in terms of boxes in which one may reside, or not. You are 'in love', 'in order', 'in conflict', 'in a position', 'in defence', etc. You cannot be both inside and outside a box – hence no two passports. And those boxes harbour an essence that you only have inside it, not outside.

But in fact, one is inside different boxes at the same time: in one's neighbourhood, in a job, in a profession, municipality, and yes, also in a country. That is paradoxical: how can you be in different boxes at the same time? Which is the box 'that really matters?' In this way thought is forced in the wrong direction. The box apparently is not a good metaphor.

An alternative is to think in terms of relations, and patterns of them, in networks. You cannot simultaneously be in different boxes but you can be in different networks. And then you have more or less overlapping networks with others, in a neighbourhood, family, friends, job, profession, etc. And then, what is more important: the neighbourhood, family, friends, province, nation, or Europe, say? You are in all at the same time, and there is nothing wrong with that. Which network is salient depends on the context. Is it about work, personal relationships, where you live, profession, religion, vacation, or home country?

And then a problem arises for the lower educated and less mobile people, who have lost their local networks of neighbourhood, church, pub and job, and received no replacement of networks in profession and globalization. It is no coincidence that they crave especially for the preservation of values of family, community and religion. They cherish the metaphor of the box for lack of networks, falling back on the intuitions of kinship and the 'in-group'.

Networks vary in their density and in the strength, durability and 'richness', i.e. multiplicity of content, of ties. In many cases ties have become less local and less rich in the sense of less personal and more formal. The content of ties can be material goods, knowledge, communication, reputation, direction, empathy, support, symbols, ritual, etc.

What maintains a network, what is its cement? That is partly economic, in shared interest and mutual complementarity, as in markets. It is also cultural: shared views, understandings, familiarity, values and norms of conduct, habits, style of conduct, etc. Those are mostly tacit, unspoken and taken for granted, requiring no argument until they are lacking. They are backed up with stories of shared history, symbolism, ideology and rituals to maintain and confirm them.

Those vary within a nation, with habitat, family,

profession, job, education, region, etc. Such identity is primarily local but can to some extent be
raised to the national level. What people primarily share, in a nation, is language, the laws that
have been made, the underlying legal constitution, with the corresponding legal institutions
and legal process. But that one also has, to a lesser
extent, in the EU. The nation does not in fact refer
to a unique property or essence, but to a shared
product.

In his book on identity, Francis Fukuyama wrote
of four characteristics of the feeling of forming a
people: shared religion, ethnicity, language and
democratic governance. Because of the mixing,
in the US, of religions and ethnicities, only the
last two remained, and for that Fukuyama used
the term of 'creedal identity': shared views of
how people associate with each other. I adopt
that notion, needed in the present mixing of
religion and ethnicity also in European societies.
It is crucial not to see identity in terms of goals in
life, but in terms of how to deal with each other,
leaving room for variety in goals. It is not about
who we are but about what we do.

An idea has run out of hand of identity, of 'who
one is', as connected to a group to which one
belongs and with which one identifies: next to religion also feminism, LGBT, environmental activ-
ism, white power, being non-white, or having a
history in slavery. The recognition of such groups
was needed for the recognition of injustice and a
striving for emancipation, but that has petrified in

identification with the group. The problem with it is that it then becomes difficult to negotiate about interests and make compromises on that: claims of identity, of 'who we are', are not negotiable.

According to a rule of thumb, there is a maximum to the size of a group that maintains its coherence on the basis of personal contacts and reputation in a gossip network, of some 150 people. Beyond that one needs either a shared hierarchy or a shared ideology, with corresponding mythology and symbolism.

Hierarchy can arise by concentration of power in central positions in networks. One can also derive identity from a political party or movement, with a political ideology. That counts the more, the more there is loss of networks of neighbourhood, community, church, job, etc., as discussed earlier. A political party is also best seen not as the container of some essence, but as a network of leaders, opinion makers and functionaries (ministers, MPs, local administrators), who contribute to shared ideology, interpretation and style, which can shift in time. There looms the danger of an elite that locks itself up in itself and thereby no longer satisfies the task of representation of an electorate, which can lead to desertion or revolt.

Collective identity is expressed in symbols. The identity that foreigners ascribe to the Dutch is symbolized by windmills, clogs, cheese and, for Americans, the little boy who stuck his thumb in the leak of a dyke, which to the Dutch is totally unknown. The nice thing about symbols, and their effectiveness, is that they are subject to a variety of interpretations, which leaves some leeway for variety. In this way, symbols can gesture towards unity while hiding a variety of views. The symbols can also be role models, such as, in the Netherlands, William of Orange, who led the rebellion against Spain in the 16th century, and the soccer player Johan Cruijff. The view of symbols can change. Jan Pieterszoon Coen, the governor of the then Dutch colony of Indonesia, once was a hero but now is a vile colonialist. Symbols are not innocent. They are part of a symbolic order that carries an ideology while at the same time occluding it.

Nationalism

In view of all this, the re-emergence of nationalism is understandable, as a craving for restoration of the local, the old, shared culture, with its own supposed essence, pseudo kinship and in-group bias. But when you look at what that means, it largely falls apart as loose sand. Is the essence of, say, the Dutch, the 'Jewish-Christian values', the Enlightenment, Romanticism or the classical Greek heritage? Protestantism or Catholicism? Wars have been waged between them. Which side between nobles and slaves, bourgeois and labour, monarchy or republic, city and countryside, high and low education?

Admittedly, nation often goes together with a

shared language, with exceptions (Switzerland). But there are also dialects, and people can communicate with different languages, at home and abroad. The state is accompanied by laws, but those increasingly, and necessarily, cross borders. Nationalists parade myths of ancient knights and resistance heroes, but on closer inspection they fall apart. And one can equally, perhaps better, identify with the local soccer club.

To an increasing extent, laws and regulations must be supra-national, concerning terrorism, the climate, migration, defence, foreign policy, control of financial markets, media, fake news, hacking, privacy, transport and ICT. That side of globalization is inevitable and beneficial.

Community

If one wants a return to the local, why not go a step deeper than the national, to municipalities or neighbourhoods, or in other words the 'commons'? Then an 'hourglass shape' arises: more on the supra-national level, less on the national level and more on the local level.

The local level approaches the scale of the original, iconic democracy in Athens, where citizens (admittedly, no women or slaves) entered in discussion with each other on the city square. There one achieves personal contact, gossip and reputation. Admittedly, this can be dominated by demagogues, but that happens on the national level as well. Also, it can derail in clientship. On the local level citizens can be involved in 'organic collaboration', policy formation with citizens' councils, election of mayors and council members, and in projects for development and implementation of policy. The rise of local parties has shown the interest in this.

An example is the municipality of Saillans in France, and another the initiative in the English municipality of Frome.[4] There, citizens, united in the movement of 'independents for Frome', wanted to set up a citizens' council, but they could not bypass the party system in place. They then founded a party with the aim of introducing the system if they obtained a majority. In 2011 they had 17 candidates of which 10 were elected, by which they obtained a majority and introduced their system. The only thing they agreed upon in advance was a procedure for deliberation with citizens, in a 'ways of working'. They showed that it worked, and in 2015 their majority rose to 17 members of the council.

What are the potential problems? Some people do not want to participate, and simply want government to take care of things. Or people drop out because they form an excluded minority. Or participation requires a level of knowledge or abstraction that they do not have. On the local level, that is not a large problem, because it often concerns local spatial planning (roads, playgrounds, bridges) or schools, care, security, or conveniences, for which one does not require higher education to form a judgement. The lower educated are no less intelligent, dedicated and socially capable but perhaps are more so.

However, also with local referenda the choices of a majority can violate the rights of a minority. Who oversees that the rule of law is not violated? Perhaps for these reasons there must be a local ombudsman where people can lodge a complaint. How about a possible danger of local clientship, where local bobos rule, misuse their power, and fall into corruption? The chance of that is no less in the present hierarchies of national parties, with deals behind doors, than in the broader, public councils we are dealing with here.

Another potential problem is the following. Decentralization entails local differences, thus inequality of facilities and arrangements. There lies a fundamental political issue: is one pre-pared to accept such differences? Must a limit be imposed on such inequalities? Where should that be done? I spoke to a mayor who implanted local governance with different outcomes in different parts of the city, and found that people could very well understand that such differences may be in order. Of course, laws remain national, with equality under the law.

A model for the economy that I am pleading for in this book may lie in the African belief and practice, in society and economy, of 'Ubuntu'. That rests on the principle that all human beings are interconnected and inter-dependent. It advo-cates and perpetuates the values of commonal-ity and reciprocity. Mary Njeri Kinyanjui (2019) sums up the business model involved as follows: 'solidarity entrepreneurialism, which encourages individual initiatives in a context of group agency ... reflected in the sharing of transaction costs ... learning from older traders and later mentoring new ones, agreeing to rules that regulate the group, and pooling assets' (p. 121). This yields what from the perspective of mainstream economics and modern corporate capitalism, adopted by the African elites, is derogated as a primitive 'informal economy', but it continues to flourish in local markets of traders and artisans. Evidence for its viability lies in the fact that it has flourished for a long time in history, before the advent of capitalism and colonialism. I haven't studied this field myself, and I hold one important reservation: the expectation that the closer local bonds of kin and solidarity are, the greater the tension between communities and tribes, which may create a lock-in into local communities and contribute to inter-tribe conflict and violence. However, Mary Njeri Kinyanjui presents evidence that in the large markets of traders and artisans in large African cities there is collaboration between tribes, taking care to share and rotate leadership among them. I think this should be given open attention and further investigation.

Banking

A discussion of the banking crisis and possible solutions cannot be left out here, because it is a paragon of how markets can go wrong, but it becomes a bit technical, here and there.

What was going on? The problems began when banks started to provide not only checking and saving accounts but also mortgages and other forms of credit, including shares, and started owning and trading them. Doing that, they fell into the temptation to take too high risks, and to hide them, as in dubious mortgages, and to hive off the risks onto the community, which is forced to rescue big banks when they are about to fail to prevent the system breakdown that would result from their default.

In the aftermath of the crisis of 2008, measures were taken to rein in the banks to some extent. In Europe that had to be done on the supranational, European level, for sufficient clout against the big banks. Among other things, banks must now hold larger reserves against risk, the calculation of risk has been regulated, a bankers' oath was instituted, and bonuses were curtailed. However, the deeper problems have not been solved. There still is the problem that one cannot let big banks default. The director of the G30,[5] Mackintosh, said: 'If a major international bank once again teeters on the brink of collapse, no one in finance believes they would be allowed to fail'(WRR, 2019, p. 131).

Mid September 2018 the president of the Dutch national bank expressed his amazement and concern that that again banks now claim a yield on investments of 15 per cent. With a riskless interest rate of about zero that can only work under excessive risks. There is a solution, in splitting up banks into low-risk public banks for checking accounts and savings, fully backed by the national bank, and banks that offer credit, investment and trade in shares and bonds, which deregulated, must carry their own risks and be allowed to default, at the expense only of owners and shareholders. Such a split was instituted in the US (in the Glass–Steagall act of 1915), but was later abolished under pressures of banking (under President Clinton), instituted again by President Obama and abolished again by President Trump. A similar proposal was recently put to the EU but rejected, for reasons unknown. Recently, in January 2019, in the Netherlands the Scientific Council for Government Policy (WRR) issued a similar proposal. Another proposal was to enhance 'relationship banking', with a role for citizen panels, for oversight and advice, and a representative from customers as member of the supervisory board.

The continuation of misconduct not only concerns banks. After scandals of tamper software in the automobile industry, it was in the news recently that now the same firms are being indicted by the EU for collusion in keeping from the market new systems that clean exhaust gases. The pharmaceutical industry demands exorbitant prices for some medication and claim that this is justified by the high costs of development in relation to the low volume of sales, but they refuse to make the costs of development and production transparent so that the claim can be tested. The joint agreement in the industry not to give that information can be seen as a form of oligopolistic collusion.

2. Economics

After a sketch of developments in society that indicate the need for a different approach to the economy and economics, here is, first, an overview of dominant economic theory and problems with it, as the basis for the later question: how could it be different?

Which economics?

As in other sciences, in economics there are different schools of thought. Here are the main ones: the mainstream of neo-classical economics, evolutionary economics, institutional economics (old and new), post-Keynesian economics, and spatial economics and economic geography. Here, to begin with I focus on the mainstream, which has had the greatest influence. The other schools, each in their own way, try to answer to the problems of the mainstream.

Here, in a nutshell, are the most important differences. The mainstream is oriented towards optimal outcomes on the basis of rational choice, evolutionary economics on processes of adaptation where optimal outcomes are seldom reached. The mainstream calculates risks but cannot deal with radical uncertainty, where one does not know in advance what can happen. This issue is further discussed later. Evolutionary economics does deal with uncertainty, in evolutionary processes without prior intelligent design.[1] One of the few economists who took on uncertainty was Keynes, and that is continued in post-Keynesian economics. While the mainstream assumes autonomous individuals make rational choices in full freedom, institutional economics is oriented at institutions, defined as humanly devised rules of the game, which enable and constrain markets and conduct more in general. Spatial economics and economic geography take into account place and space, which in the mainstream are mostly disregarded.

The core of economics

What are the headlines of the mainstream? How can one represent a school of thought? That is more than any single theory: a set of theories with shared points of departure and approach. For that, Imre Lakatos (1978) offered the idea of a *research programme*. That has a *hard core* of fundamental assumptions, directions for research, and methodological principles, which at all costs must be protected against refutation, in *falsification*. That is done on the basis of a *protective belt* of subsidiary assumptions that help to yield different content derived from the core. If facts arise that contradict a theory in the programme, they are attributed to a shortcoming in the protective belt, not the core, and a replacement or extension is sought to redress the problem.

Isn't such tenacity in holding on to a programme unscientific? Indeed, it can get bogged down there, but there are two arguments for it. One is economic: if something has worked well, one does not renounce it at the first, merest imperfection. You don't drop it until its failure turns out to be systematic. The second argument comes from theory of knowledge. Every theory necessarily is an abstraction; it leaves things out to obtain focus and make it tractable. One cannot explain everything in one go. By holding on to a programme one finds out where its real strengths and limits lie, and one collects indications in what direction to seek a change. That is a form of progressive conservatism.

If anyone does not like it, he/she can set up a new, competing programme. That is what I am doing with this book. It happened in the set-up of evolutionary economics (in which I participated). There lies the strongest competition in science: not within programmes but between competing ones with different perspectives. However, competing programmes tend to ignore each other because they do not understand each other, and cannot afford to, not to spoil their own game.

The two most frequent characterizations of economics, by economists themselves, are the following: the first is optimal allocation of scarce resources in satisfying needs, the second is exchange, in particular in markets. The two are connected. Specialization in what one is good at gives an enormous push to efficiency, in division of labour, and that requires exchange. Also, the market yields competition, which exerts pressure on efficiency. That appears in the core of the mainstream, as follows:

> *Rational choice by autonomous actors, in the calculation of optimal choice, on the basis of given preferences, and the operation of markets that bring equilibrium between supply and demand. The protective belt supplies particulars concerning technology, production and consumption, laws (as of property), communication, and transport.*

The toolbox

Next to the central mission (optimal choice) and the core of the programme, there is a toolbox of concepts that are useful in whatever programme. Here are a few.

There is the idea of *diminishing returns*. Often the extra ('marginal') utility of something declines as one has more of it. There is saturation; urgency declines. That does not always arise. In addiction one wants more and more. That also applies to greed: every time a need is fulfilled, new needs arise, one remains dissatisfied and wants more, and thus greed builds on itself. And if ever one were satisfied, boredom would strike. That applies also to power: power evokes counterpower and must then increase to deal with that. Power needs to strengthen itself to remain in power.

There is the idea of *opportunity* costs: if one

spends on something, what does one give up, surrendering the opportunity to spend it on something else?

There is the idea of *economies of scale*: the efficiency of something (e.g. production) increases to the extent that there is more of it. Mostly, only the advantages are seen, which leads to an increase of scale which has implications for competition by concentration in fewer, large firms. There are several forms of scale effect. There is the 'pot-and-pan' effect: the content of a sphere, such as a reactor vat in the chemical industry, or the body of a jumbo jet, is proportional to the third degree of the radius, while the circumference is proportional to the square of the radius. Revenue is proportional to content (amount of chemicals, number of passengers), while cost is proportional to surface (material costs, weight and transportation costs, cleaning, heat loss, air resistance). Then the ratio between revenue and cost is proportional to the radius and thus increases with size.

For an illustration, consider the following. Why are warm-blooded animals at the North Pole (polar bears, walruses, whales) large and globular? Because then the loss of heat through the surface is less, relative to the production of heat in the body. But then, how come there are also large globular animals around the equator (elephants, rhinos, hippos)? Because it is about the difference of temperature inside and outside, also when the latter is hotter than the former. When big and globular you absorb relatively less heat.

But why, then, are there also thin, lean animals around the equator (pumas, leopards)? Because in the explosion of exertion to sprint after prey, internal heat exceeds external heat, and needs to be radiated out.

Other advantages of size, called *economies of scope*, are efficiencies from combining different activities, in sharing costs, joint utilization of capacity (administration, ICT, a distribution channel, a shop, legal expertise, etc.), or mutual complementarity: for clapping one needs two hands, and to lift a closet two pairs of hands. Advantages arise from the combination of specializations in innovative 'novel combinations', and the spread of risk across different activities (different products, different markets).

However, there are also limits and disadvantages to size, and those are often neglected. The advantage of scale tapers off at larger size (decreasing returns), and above a certain scale one does not gain much more. There are also disadvantages of large scale. With more people there are more opportunities for contact between them: they increase with the square of the number of people.[2] If all those opportunities are realized one no longer gets to work. That leads to the classical solution of a hierarchy: contacts are limited according to hierarchical level. That leads to divergence between high and low, between management and work floor.

Another economy of volume is that of experience, as a function of aggregate volume in time, which yields an increase of expertise. An example arises in health care, where surgeons are required to conduct a certain operation a minimum number of times a year.

The notion of substitutes and complements is also useful. Labour and capital are both needed, complements, with labour using tools and installations, but technology can also lead to labour being replaced by capital (e.g. in the use of robots). In relationships, control and trust complement each other, but more trust yields more room for less control. They are both complements and substitutes.

Mathematics

Many mainstream economists pride themselves on using mathematics, as the paragon of scientific virtue. The opportunity for it arises from the orientation towards optimal outcomes, which one can derive mathematically from a utility function under side conditions. However, that often requires assumptions which are insufficiently realistic, whereby the value of the model as representation of reality becomes dubious. The question should always be how great that deviation is, and on what points, and how bad that is given the purpose of the analysis.

I have an illustration from my own experience, with a model of innovation as a race for who achieves discovery first. The chance of discovery is modelled according to a certain probability distribution (the 'Poisson' distribution, which was first used for the chance that a Prussian cavalryman got kicked to death by a horse). In the model, that chance is affected by the size of investment in innovation. The prize of winning the race is also assumed to be known. It was an elegant little model, and the outcomes accorded well with the empirical data. Yet at second sight I rejected the model. Innovation is uncertain, and how then do you know in advance what the revenue and the probability distribution of success is? The model could still apply if it is about incremental innovation, the improvement of what exists, but the research was about radical innovation. So, I experienced myself how great the temptation can be to make such assumptions, and to crowbar reality into the model.

However, unrealistic models are not necessarily misleading. They can be admittedly unrealistic but useful to clarify the logic of a causal argument. The model of an optimum can also be useful, not with the pretence that it fits, but as a 'benchmark' with which more realistic accounts can be contrasted.

Developments

In the mainstream there have been several quite fundamental changes and additions. Two are mentioned here.

First, *game theory*, which by the way is not a theory but a method, gives a method for the analysis of strategic interaction between actors. There, one has a set of possible strategies and a matrix of 'pay-offs' for the actors involved, for combinations of strategies. One then seeks the best strategy, taking into account responses that actors have to each other's choice. Where does that lead? Economists seek equilibrium, and here that is found in the 'Nash equilibrium': the choice of a strategy is stable, and hence viable, if for each participant it is the best, given the choices of all the others. That, with its variants, gives a powerful method. It still rests on the aim for optimal choice. The underlying assumption is that the set of strategies and their outcomes are given. Unfortunately, that is often not the case, where they emerge during or after choices are made and executed (they are 'emergent').

A later, more fundamental change was that of *behavioural economics*, based on insights from social psychology. That changes the basic assumption of rational choice, in recognizing that people make choices on the basis of often non-rational decision *heuristics*,[3] shortcuts to decisions that are not per se irrational but mostly do not lead to optimal choice. Examples will be given later in this book. A methodological advantage is that this is amenable to experiments, often of teachers with students.

However, it does not sit easily with the core of the programme, in departing from rational choice. From collaboration between applied psychologists and economists in this area I hear the complaint from the former that the latter cannot desist from forcing the heuristics in the frame of rational choice. That is how the hard core of a programme works.

Behavioural economics has spawned a new field of *nudging*. There, in the communication of government with citizens (and firms with customers), the heuristics are taken into account to frame communication in such a way that choices are 'nudged' to get closer to optimal, in the interest of the citizen. The paradigm case is the route planner: the traveller specifies the destination, and the system nudges him/her to take the best route to get there, but he/she can deviate from it. There is an inherent danger of this sliding into manipulation, but in many cases it makes sense and is appreciated by customers.

Risk and uncertainty

As noted earlier, there is a distinction in economics between risk and (more fundamental) uncertainty. With risk one does not know what *will* happen, but one does know what *can* happen. And then one can append probabilities to calculate optimal choice, in the form of maximum expected utility (sum of probabilities × outcomes). With uncertainty, by contrast, that is not the case. What can happen often becomes clear only later, after the choice is made.

And there the economist stands empty-handed, and cannot perform his art of calculation, and therefore he/she is tempted to ignore uncertainty. But in innovation and in relations such uncertainty is routine. They produce the surprise of the new that goes beyond existing knowledge, ideas and imagination. The most productive relations are often the most uncertain. Often one even has no idea how one will oneself respond to relations. In economic language: preferences are endogenous. Here economics severely limits itself. If the most valuable relations are the most uncertain, then in dodging uncertainty one surrenders opportunities for value creation, and that is a very un-economic thing to do.

An exception in economics was Keynes, who did acknowledge uncertainty and used it to explain herd effects in the economy, which account for bubbles and their burst: if one cannot calculate optimal choice, then it is not unreasonable to follow what others do, even if that turns out to be arbitrary, especially as opinion leaders claim to be experts who do know.

Evolutionary economics takes uncertainty into account: evolution is not based on prior 'intelligent design' but on trial and error, and selection of what survives in markets and institutions. It is aimed not at optimization but at adaptation.

A methodological sleight of hand

The mainstream bases itself on the following fundamental assumptions: economic actors are autonomous, have given and known preferences, and make rational, optimal decisions in the spending of scarce resources to satisfy those preferences. That is not a realistic claim, and good economists readily admit that such actors do not exist. People are in fact limitedly rational and routinely make non-optimal choices. The assumptions are a fiction, but according to the methodology of *instrumentalism* they serve as instruments for a sparse, rigorous deduction of phenomena. That saves enormously on the effort and complexity of describing the real choices of people, which is the domain of psychology, in interaction with each other, which is the domain of sociology, not economics.

This is not nonsense. A theory is always an abstraction and simplification. If it were as complex as observed reality it would not serve its purpose. And even beyond science, every view is mediated, enabled and simultaneously constrained by a certain perspective, a way of looking and interpreting, which mostly one is not even aware of. One acts 'as if' the tacit assumptions are correct, and then waits to see what comes out. The justification of this is the theory leads to implications or predictions that can be empirically tested.

The scientific scandal of economics now is that this can hardly be done, for two reasons. In the first place, predictions have effects on conduct that produce the outcomes, and can thereby be self-fulfilling or self-destructive. In the second place, in economics there is little opportunity for controlled experiments where one can control the conditions that have effects in addition to the effects one claims from the theory. Society is not a laboratory. One can retrodict what has happened, to see if the theory can explain it, but one cannot control all factors. That then yields the so-called *ceteris paribus* problem: the pre- or retrodictions are valid only if all factors not controlled for remain constant, while one knows this is not the case. Furthermore, often relevant variables are difficult or impossible to measure, which is needed to include them in the calculation. But because there is the imperative of measurement, research limits itself to what is measurable, thus leaving out what may be the most important variables. That yields the following joke. In the middle of the night a man stands leaning against a lamp post, staring at the ground. A passer-by asks 'Why are you standing there?' 'I am looking for my car keys.' 'Did you lose them there?' 'No, but the light is here.'

And then, and here lies the real scandal, economists perform the following sleight of hand. They begin with the admission that their assumptions are false, next cannot perform a hard test of the predictions, and then proceed to act as if the assumptions are certain, reliable and scientific. And the argument is so alluring. One goes back to the lesson from Adam Smith about the 'invisible hand'. Every consumer seeks satisfaction of his/her own desires, that creates a demand, and if supply cannot serve it, prices go up, to attract more supply, until there is equilibrium between supply and demand. Thus, by an invisible hand resources are directed to where they yield the greatest utility in satisfaction of demand. Hence the market is good and should be applied everywhere.

Evolution

An illustration that has been offered of the instrumentalism of optimal choice is the following. From Chicago (the crucible of market economics) cars drive in arbitrary directions. There are gas stations only along some of the roads. After some time cars are moving only along roads with gas stations. So it is as if those drivers chose those roads rationally. The idea is that competition in markets takes care that only those choices survive that were efficient. Therefore, we can argue as if observed actions are rational and optimal. They are the only ones visible.

A reply to this[4] was that if the argument is in fact one of selection of what survives, by markets, one should model that process of selection by the market. And then it will show up how efficient, in fact, markets are in selecting out suboptimal choices. And thus one arrives at *evolutionary economics*. However, that gets complicated in modelling complex processes, dependent on many conditions, where economics loses its crystalline clarity and rigour that forms its pride; the pride of a myth of equilibria without any account of the processes by which they are or are not achieved.

For an illustration, here is an anecdote. Some

time ago I was member of an advisory council for a Max Planck Institute for evolutionary economics in Jena, Germany. In a periodic evaluation of the institute there was criticism from mainstream economics: the results of research were not unified and too complex, not up to the analytical clarity of the mainstream. The institute did not survive the evaluation, and was re-staffed by the mainstream.

Forms of efficiency

Economics recognizes three forms of efficiency: allocative, productive and dynamic. Allocative efficiency forms the core of market thinking – scarce resources are optimally allocated to where demand is highest. Productive efficiency concerns the efficiency of production, which depends, among other things, on the scale of firms. Dynamic efficiency is efficiency in dynamics, innovation. All three are desirable, and are adduced as arguments for markets, but they are in each other's way. Increase of scale can yield more productive efficiency, but also less competition, which is in the way of allocative efficiency. Dynamic efficiency is the most difficult, because of the uncertainty involved, which economics does not deal with. Because of uncertainty, one needs reserves to absorb failures, but for allocative efficiency those should not be there.

In the innovation literature there is a long-running discussion, still going on, on whether large or small firms are the most innovative.

Large firms have the advantage of more financial resources, spread of risk, specialists and lobbying power, with influence on regulation, markets, standards and more. That obstructs allocative efficiency. Firms with large sales of existing products have an interest in a delay of the 'creative destruction' of radical innovation, to prolong the economic life of existing products and corresponding investments. That obstructs dynamic efficiency. Smaller, new, entrepreneurial firms lack the scale advantages of size and experience, but are more flexible, are not tied to vested interests of established products and investments, and are flexible, efficient also in their demise: if the venture fails, so does the firm; it is not kept alive.

Which form of efficiency carries the most weight? Small and large can complement each other. When an innovation survives design and tests, there often arises a 'valley of death': a long haul with pitfalls of further development, set-up of production, marketing and distribution, and scaling up, and there large firms are often better, with their experience, contacts and advantages of scale. A good model then is that the small firm transfers its innovation to a large firm, and then turns to the next innovation. That happens, for example, in biotechnology.

Ethics

There is debate about whether ethics should play a larger role, to curtail misconduct, e.g. at banks.

There, courses in ethics are now given, and a bankers' oath has been introduced. Even right-leaning liberals now grant that discussion about ethics is needed, while for liberals ethics used to be something exclusively for the private sphere.

Economists often claim that they do not act on the basis of value judgements, but only indicate what the economic consequences are of policies. But the theory they employ does have an implicit ethics, even if they are not aware of it. Of what kind is that ethic?

There are several ethical systems. Liberalism, and thereby mainstream economic science, is based on utility ethics. That is a form of ethics that only looks at outcomes of choices and actions; here utility, prosperity for the greatest number. The ethical quality of other considerations and goals of action, such as honesty, justice and compassion are not relevant. 'Greed is good' as long as it leads to higher prosperity, and the justice of the distribution of that is less relevant.

That stands in sharp contrast with duty ethics, going back to the philosopher Kant, which is about the ethical quality of motives of actions, apart from their outcomes. The claim is that ethical rules are universal, valid everywhere and under all circumstances. The central rule is that of the *categorical imperative*: an act is good if one wants it to be raised to a general rule. That derives from the much older *Golden Rule*, operating long before Christ, in many parts in the world (Armstrong, 2006): you must (not) treat other people in the way that you would (not) want to be treated yourself. Lying is good if you want everyone to do it. You don't want that, so you don't lie. I do not go along with the imperative, because what I find good you may not, and what is good or bad depends on circumstances.

A third system is virtue ethics, going back to the philosopher Aristotle. Virtues are character traits, dispositions to conduct. Many virtues may enter, depending on circumstances. Classical virtues are those of prudence, courage, moderation and justice. There is nothing intrinsically wrong with pleasure and enjoyment, but within reason and boundaries of the virtues. That is sorely lacking in the present theory and practice of economics.

For moderation, consider the following paradox: within prosperous countries over the last 50 years happiness, measured as being satisfied with life, has hardly increased, despite the huge increase in the standard of living. People adjust their expectations and desires to the level of prosperity reached.

Prudence, reason and reasonability are needed to act on the basis of arguments, courage is needed to face and accept risks and uncertainties, moderation is needed to limit the escalation of desire and power, and justice is needed as a basis for sharing and including others. As the revolt against some large firms, such as banks and pharmaceutical companies, increases, it is beginning to hurt those firms, and increasingly they come with proposals for self-regulation. The question then is whether if push comes to shove and it leads to less profit, it will be accepted by shareholders. For that I give an anecdote. Some time ago I was approached by a colleague in Glasgow as to whether I would be willing to contribute, as advisor and possibly as an instructor, for a bank in the training/education of staff in trustworthiness. Trust is one of my subjects, so I accepted. The first step was a Skype meeting for an exploration of ideas. We came to an agreement and I was asked to develop a proposal. In the discussion of that, I asked whether it was also the intention to educate staff in trustworthiness with regard to customers, not to offer opaque products that could be to their disadvantage, as was customary during the crisis of 2008. I received no answer, and the discussion was abruptly ended. I tried to get in the comment that if you were the only bank to achieve that, this would probably be very profitable, but they had already signed off.

Earlier in this book, I pleaded for attention to African practices of 'Ubuntu' in the economy. Again, I quote Mary Njeri Kinyanjui (2019, p. 121): 'It is driven by a spirit of solidarity as well as courage, endurance, resilience . . .'. That appears to come close to the ethics that I plead for in this book.

Political economy

In economics it used to be routine, in 'political economy', to link considerations of income and economic growth with the consideration of an equitable distribution of income. In the transition in the 1980s from a Keynesian economics of demand management to an economics of the 'supply side' of business and markets, the issue of distributive justice dropped out from the equations, and the political dropped out from economics. How could this disappearing act have been pulled off? It was because economics was based on a utility ethic: looking only at outcomes, in terms of utility, as the greatest prosperity for the greatest number of people, without regard for values such as the quality of society, motives, goals, intentions and justice, in contrast with Kantian ethics. With that, politics dropped out from economics, because politics is concerned with those other values, such as justice, community and compassion.

I think that here lies a deeper motive behind the present populist revolt: a sense that economics has passed by the most important things in life. Economists have buried themselves in their stance that they make no value judgements but only analyse the objective conditions and outcomes of political or managerial policy. This is the technocratic hideaway that is mistrusted in feelings of disenfranchisement: people sense other values but see that they have no grip on them and see them slip through their fingers.

This populist turn away from economics is dangerous if the pendulum swings too far away from economic considerations of scarcity, efficiency and the trade needed for it. We need to build a new political economy that attends to economic conditions as well as the political exigencies of values beyond utility. For that, in this book I plead for the replacement, in a new economics, of the utility ethic by a virtue ethic which includes pragmatic economic considerations as well as, and in combination with, the classical virtues of prudence, courage, moderation and justice.

Greed and urge of manifestation

Discussions of capitalism are usually about greed: the urge for profit and income. But perhaps more important is the urge 'to make a difference', to stand out, and to gain glamour and attention.

The philosopher Plato spoke of reason as a charioteer who had to restrain two horses: the horse of *eros*, lust for acquisition, and *thymos*, the urge for self-manifestation. The philosopher Nietzsche proposed that the urge for power is stronger than the urge for survival. Spinoza used the similar notion of *conatus* as the basic drive of humans. One can appreciate that; it is also the urge of ambition, of 'making something out of your life', including the 'making of a contribution to society'. That is also, more than profit, the main drive of entrepreneurs. They feel themselves underrated when set aside as 'grabbers'.

The overall outcome of a mountain of research on happiness is that it mostly consists of a combination of 'pleasure and purpose', with purpose as a form of transcendence; rising above oneself for the sake of something bigger, i.e. *transcendence*. That can be vertical, oriented at God or heaven, but also horizontal, towards society. It is not necessarily about immortality for yourself, but a contribution to what you leave behind after death. And if in that you utilize your talents, that is even pleasurable. It is also not only about outcomes, as the economist thinks, but also about the intrinsic value of activity, and of virtue: you feel you do this because that is who you are. The joy of life is to have pleasure in things that are produced with pleasure. But there is also intrinsic value in following conviction. The urge for manifestation can also be a virtue, in simply being good at something, and virtue ethics makes room for that, provided it is accompanied, or combined, with the virtues of reason, moderation and justice.

However, money and influence are both addictive, for managers hunting for ever higher positions, stars hunting for glamour, or scientists hunting for publications and citations. I know this from my own experience.

Freedom

Liberalism and capitalism pride themselves on the freedom they offer. And indeed they offer a form of freedom: freedom from interference, to go your own way. That has been called 'negative freedom', in the denial and the absence of constraint. There is also 'positive freedom', in having access to the resources and competencies to deploy activities.[5]

For a broader look than only economic prosperity, the 'Human Development Index' now includes, next to economic performance, a long and healthy life, access to knowledge and a decent standard of living. In name, liberalism also pleads for such values: equal access to markets, information, education, politics (electing and being elected), freedom of speech, justice, etc. In fact, equality of access is limited by entry barriers to markets, professions, jobs, education, housing, networks of contacts and by limited capacities.

Socialism occupied itself with that, with all manner of government measures of subsidy, support and other aid. Then it transpired that measures were misused, in fraud, which was also seen as non-solidary, and the insight rose that support can render people dependent and passive, which is not good for themselves either. The liberal view that people should take responsibility for themselves gained force, and social measures started to crumble. Now it is seen that this in its turn went too far, and that many do need support, and not everyone is misusing it. Solidarity is returning on the agenda.

In the large literature on freedom several levels of freedom have been recognized, in addition to the two types, positive and negative freedom, indicated above. Next to those outside freedoms, from interference and of access, there are inside freedoms and unfreedoms of the will. One can have freedom of action but be carried away by unconscious drives, impulse, instinct and addiction.

There then is a 'higher' freedom, on the basis of self-reflection and control. Here one has the freedom to ask oneself what one should want, in accordance with a 'higher' will. The question then is not 'what do I want?', but 'what should I want?'. However, freedom on this level does not necessarily imply that what one would want to want is indeed good. That may be a matter of self-deception or indoctrination. One can exert self-discipline to do evil – in a terrorist act, for example, for which one renounces comfort and safety.

Take the case of Kim Jong-un, the present ruler of North Korea. Is he a cold, ruthless, psychopathic, narcissic dictator who deliberately mistreats and destroys his own people? Or does he firmly believe that what he is doing is good, because he has been spoon-fed on it, isolated from the rest of the world? Or is he captive in a maze of power play, manoeuvres and intrigue in which he personally seeks to survive?

The freedom of self-reflection is not as evident as it may seem. Here we run up against the debate on the existence or not of free will. Neurological research and social psychology have shown how dominant the unconscious is in our choices and actions, in unconscious impulse, intuition and feelings, which often yield surprisingly effective decisions.

A next level of freedom is that of self-perfection, to change what one wants and believes is good, in a shift of views on right and wrong. The question then is where that would come from. An important source is the Christian morality of self-control, moderation, benevolence and help for the weak. Nietzsche rejected that with great gusto, as hypocritical and inimical to human flourishing, in false self-denial, and suppression of the forces of life, creativity and excellence.

A fourth level of freedom is that of transforming oneself, in a revaluation of all values, a shift of convictions concerning the good and the bad on level three. Nietzsche believed in it. It is also an ideal of a form of romanticism: transcending boundaries, breaking out. Many think that one cannot achieve this level, because everyone is determined by genetic potential plus experience along one's path of life, and character that blossoms from this. The image dawns of the Baron of Münchhausen who lifts himself from the swamp by his own bootstraps. I will now argue that this highest level of freedom can be achieved, up to a point, but not on one's own. To have a chance for it, one needs opposition from the other.

Self and other

The economist assumes that the individual is autonomous, and that all action is to be analysed from that perspective, in 'methodological individualism'. In fact, however, the individual is socially constituted: he/she develops his/her thought and action in interaction with his/her environment. Thought guides that action but is also formed in it. Preferences also are not all given in advance but are formed in experience in what emerges in action. Consequently, people are still individuals, but not autonomous, fundamentally concerned with each other, in their development. That gives a radically different perspective from that of the economic mainstream.

If interaction with others is not just normative, something one is supposed to do, but formative, contributing to development of the self, then this enhances it as a central virtue to take others into account, and to empathize with them. That is also to the benefit of yourself. It is also needed to practice the virtues of prudence, moderation, and justice.

In sum, one needs the other not only for economic reasons, for the efficiency of division of labour, but also for reasons of freedom of knowledge and spirit. The highest level of freedom is freedom from prejudice, transcendence of the blindness of the self to itself. One will never completely achieve that, but opposition from the other is needed to stand a chance.

Here also lies the story of the master and the slave (from Hegel). The master ultimately loses out because he can impose his views and choices, while the slave must listen and adjust, and learns from it. This demands openness to the other, in radical fashion, not only to add to what you already have, but to get what you did not have – not only opening the door of your existing house, but letting in the other to help in the construction of it. There lies the inspiration from the philosophy of Emmanuel Levinas.[6] This brings along radical uncertainty, as discussed earlier: you don't know in advance what the other could bring in, because then you would already have it. And that requires the virtue of courage: the leap in the dark. This touches upon the big issue of trust, which I will not fully discuss here.

Trust is difficult to fit into mainstream economic theory, among other things because of this issue of uncertainty. You don't know all possible responses from the other, and not even your own. Then trust is a leap in the dark, a leap of faith. And as indicated earlier: the economist cannot deal with that. Trust requires give and take where you know what you give but not what you will get. The economist says that you cannot afford that under the pressure of competition in markets: there you must grab all you can get, not to lose out to others. I turn it around: innovation is needed to survive in a new market. There, collaboration with others is needed but uncertain, and if you dare not deal with that you will not survive. Economics assumes that markets produce innovation, but innovation takes place where there is no market yet.

System tragedy

Earlier, I briefly mentioned 'system tragedy': people are carried along in practices that in their hearts they condemn, because they are more or less forced to go along, by the position or role they have in a system of entangled interests, carried by an ideology or excuse that 'this is the way things go around here'. A comment of a banker during the 2008 crisis was: 'As long as the music plays, you must dance along'.

One way of looking at this is that of a 'prisoner's dilemma': you would like to act differently, but can afford to do so only if others, in particular your rivals, do so as well. Everyone thinks that and thus nothing changes and people lock each other up in misconduct. During the banking crisis, if you did not go along with the bank you would have no career. It applied on the level of banks, if you did not play along that implied that you would leave opportunities for profit unused, and that would not be forgiven by shareholders. They would then replace you as CEO or your bank would be taken over by less scrupulous rivals.

The solution is intervention by government, to impose proper conduct. That worked, for example, in limiting tobacco advertisements. That was largely wasted money, because people did not smoke more for it, but as a producer you had to take part not to lose market share. With prohibition that was resolved, and profits rose all around.

But with banks the prisoner's dilemma also plays out on the level of countries. If as a single country you impose restraints, then banks will move to a more lenient country. Thus one must take action together, on some supranational level, such as that of the EU, as has been done in the so-called Basel Agreements. If one does not do something about the systemic effects, a mere course in ethics for bankers by itself will not make the difference. It will just sharpen the sense of guilt, without altering conduct.

A different approach is the following. Recall the earlier discussion of identity. There is personal identity in the beliefs, convictions and ethics one has, and cultural identity, which I proposed to see in terms of the relations and networks one is in. The position and role one has in a system then constitutes that side of identity, and defection from the system constitutes a threat to that. Thus a conflict arises between the personal and the cultural side of identity. It then requires the virtue of courage to no longer play along and step out.

Value of difference

Here I present a lesser known piece of economics, concerning the value of difference.

People differ, in outlook, habits, knowledge, capabilities, culture and language. That is a bother if one needs to collaborate. But difference also presents the opportunity for the 'novel combinations' of innovation. And, as discussed earlier, one has blind spots and prejudices. To get away from those one needs knowledge, insight and wisdom from others. So, difference is good for change of thought and action. But how much? Difference can be too large or too small. Here I employ a

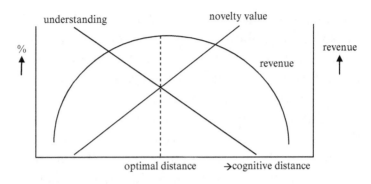

Figure 2.1   Optimal distance

simple model from my own work (Nooteboom, 2000); see Figure 2.1.

Along the horizontal axis runs 'cognitive distance', i.e. difference in knowledge, insight, skill, but also in morality, views of proper conduct. From left to right a line runs downward, indicating that as distance increases, the ability to understand and collaborate declines. By contrast, the potential of novelty increases with distance, but the ability to realize that potential declines. Actual revenue is the mathematical product of potential and ability to utilize it, and the product of the two lines is a U-shaped curve, a parabola in fact, with a maximum at a distance that is large enough to yield novelty but not so large as to prevent its grasp. The model applies not only to individuals but also to firms. On that level, difference has been measured as difference in technological profile (deduced from patents used).[7]

The line that declines, from left to right, in the ability to grasp, is not fixed, but is built up from accumulated technological knowledge and experience in collaboration with others who think differently. With such accumulation, the line shifts upwards, whereby the intersection of the two lines, at optimal distance, shifts to the right: optimal distance increases. That is good news not only economically but also politically: experience in collaborating with people who think differently yields economic advantage and thereby is politically more viable.

Here I make use of a mathematical model. Is that justifiable here? In seeking a partner for collaboration, do parties indeed establish and estimate the two lines to calculate their intersection? No, of course not. The model serves to show the logic of the argument, and clarify it. In reality, I propose, by trial and error people/firms approach the optimum: they try out small and large distances until they find where it works best. The model lends substance to the popular claim of 'open innovation', that one should not try to innovate by oneself but in collaboration with others with other knowledge or competence. The model shows both the potential of that and the problems involved, and how to reconcile them.

One can see the model as an economic model, of collaboration between firms, in particular in innovation, and that is where it was used, but also as a political model, in dealing with refugees, for example. They yield an advantage, in cultural distance, and one can benefit from it. But distance can be too large to bridge and should not be so large that mutual understanding cannot be achieved, but is also a matter of experience and courage. A minimum amount of acculturation is needed. Also, I propose, the model may contribute to the wider issue of unity in diversity in the EU, with sufficient coherence among member states but room for national differences: try to find optimal levels of difference.

The line that declines, from left to right, indicates the ability to bridge difference. That can be difference in knowledge but also in morality, in views of how people should deal with each other. In the art of bridging there are two sides of the coin: the ability to understand the other ('absorptive capacity') and the ability to help the other to understand one. The first requires openness, receptivity. The second requires rhetorical ability, in understanding what the other can and cannot understand (empathy), and inventive use of metaphor and images to help the other understand. Both depend on accumulated experience, and variety of it, in dealing with others who think and feel differently. That is not getting better, in present society, where people harness themselves in their self-justification. That is furthered in the use of social media, where people appear to lock themselves up in 'filter bubbles'.

3. Markets

Markets are indispensable, but their functioning is less simple and self-evident than many think. Markets are used both too often and too little. Too little, in limits to competition, and too often, where market imperfections are too large or markets cross moral boundaries.

Why markets?

A market is a place – virtual, via the internet, or real, some location – where supply and demand meet. That is needed for the division of labour that forms the largest source of prosperity, as Adam Smith taught. Markets also serve as a platform for competition, and that, so the theory goes, gives an incentive to efficiency.

There is also something more fundamental behind it, as proposed by Friedrich von Hayek (1937), one of the godfathers of neoliberalism. He overestimated the working of markets and underestimated their problems, but he was right concerning the fundamental value of them. He called competition a 'discovery process'. People locally know best what they need and what they can do, and in the decentralized buzz of markets optimal use is made of such local knowledge.

In the detail, differentiation and adaptability of products, central planning cannot begin to equal that.

There are fundamental objections to other aspects of economic theory, but this point remains standing. It has been proven mathematically that under certain conditions markets yield an optimal general equilibrium. When there is shortage of supply, prices rise to elicit new supply, until equilibrium is reached. A condition is that in all markets there is perfect competition, i.e. no single participant can influence prices, which arise from equilibrium of total supply and demand. Conduct is rational and self-interested, on the basis of given preferences, where individuals are anonymous and do not influence each other's preferences and choices.

These conditions are clearly unrealistic. Increasing prices may yield the expectation that they will keep rising, so that it is advantageous to wait a bit with new supply, to benefit from further price rises. That is currently happening in the housing market. In many cases there are not many anonymous buyers and sellers but few, in strategic interaction with each other, whose preferences, choices, actions, knowledge, competencies and technologies affect each other.

There are further conditions, such as the availability of information and ability to process it, to make rational choices, issues of ownership, free entry and exit from markets, and so-called transaction costs, to be discussed below. A problem also arises when there are economies of scale, which is often the case, which are in the way of perfect competition, as argued before.

Markets do not operate automatically but require institutions. Trade requires property law. Establishment at a location requires land rights. Labour requires laws against exploitation. Risks of trade and production required the invention of limited liability to spread risks. Invention requires patents, as a deliberate, temporary limit to competition. While markets require ownership laws, markets also break them down, as in music and text, as a consequence of internet. Technical standards are needed, for security, communication, configuration in buildings and instruments, trade, money and payment.

In the most general terms, conditions for markets are conditions for freedom of choice and initiative of users and producers. In as far as the conditions are not satisfied, and to a greater or lesser extent that is always the case, there are market imperfections. Then regulation is needed, and one can reach a point where regulation limits freedom to such an extent that one can ask whether one can still speak of markets. And this raises the question if then public planning and control may not be better.

Earlier, I characterized the advantages of markets in three notions: variation and local specificity of knowledge/information, incentives of self-interest, and competition. Let us consider each in turn.

Freedom for users goes much further than the formal availability of alternatives to choose from. The user must not only have the opportunity of choice, but also the ability for it, to judge difference, and to switch without costs to an alternative. This leads to a consideration of the notion of 'transaction costs'.

Transaction costs

Markets carry costs. Those are so-called transaction costs, in the connection between supply and demand, of *contact*, *contract* and *control*.[1] Transaction cost theory is now a standard part of economics. Here I explain the notion.

Costs of contact are costs of searching and judging quality and reliability. The producer seeks and solicits users, for example in advertising. The user seeks and compares suppliers, e.g. via internet. The question then is to what extent the user can judge differences in quality. To maximize profit, the supplier has an interest in exaggerating quality and hiding problems, e.g. in 'small print' and misleading advertising. One can increase profit also by differentiating one's product from competing products, often in semblance more than in substance. Differentiated products yield more profit than a product identical to that of a competitor. The argument adduced for advertising is that it lowers search costs for users. Yes, but it is also used for bogus differentiation. One can also combine products (including services) in one package, in 'salami tactics', so that they cannot be obtained separately, such as hardware and software, for example, with patent protection on one of them, which then also covers what is connected with it.

If anything qualifies for the good operation of a market it is raw materials, because they are reasonably homogeneous and hence in direct competition, while differences can be competently judged by professional buyers. However, with regard to consumers even something as basically homogeneous as gasoline is presented as differentiated, with bogus claims, logos with their colours and brand image.

Costs of contract lie in the making of an agreement or contract, and other ways of managing risks in relations, such as dependence. A contract presupposes that one knows what to control, and how. As uncertainty increases that becomes more problematic. This arises especially in innovation, the essence of which being that there must be room for surprise. If one nails everything down for the sake of a closed contract, that becomes a straitjacket that obstructs the purpose of surprise. Then one must turn to other instruments for managing relational risk. That will be discussed later, in Chapter 5 on a new programme for economics.

Thirdly, there are costs of control, of the conformance to agreements. A contract does not make sense if one lacks knowledge and insight in that. To what extent does one have insight in the quality of performance? Hierarchy falters as more and more use is made of professional workers because they can do something you cannot, and it becomes paradoxical to assume that you can judge it, let alone prescribe what is to be done and how. That has important implications for the task of oversight and control. That will also be discussed further in Chapter 5.

An important concept here is that of 'relation-specific investments', taken from the theory of transaction costs. Those are investments one can recoup only in the relationship for which they were made. If the relation breaks those are lost and one needs to make them again, but differently, in a different relationship. Thus, they make for dependence. The partner can use it to put pressure on the investor to yield a greater share of returns: 'if you don't give me more, I will walk, and you lose your investment'. Examples of specific investments are machines, installations, instruments, training and buildings specially designed or located for the relationship, but also the gathering of knowledge concerning the partner organization: who is who, who does what, where the power lies, and the building of trust. And the connection between the two: trust in people depends on their position in the organization. Specific investment also arises in labour relations – workers and management make themselves dependent by taking or giving training specific for the firm or the worker.

Concerning the judgement of a product, the following typology is used:

- Search products: one can judge quality before use, such as cars, washing machines, houses, etc.
- Experience products: one can judge quality during consumption, such as restaurants, musical shows, films, hotels, holidays, books, etc.
- Credence products: one cannot judge quality even after use, such as car repair, tax consultant, doctor, course, etc.

The vulnerability and dependence of the user increase from top to bottom. The supplier can exploit that, with misleading or vacuous advertising or information. One tries to turn experience goods into search goods, more or less, with reviews or client response. One can also build brand name as the basis for trust.

A credence good can be partly an experience good: a course may be more or less pleasant, clear and entertaining, but if one could judge its substantive value one would no longer need the course. In health care the demeanour of the doctor, his/her communication and readiness to listen, may distract from what really matters: his/her competence. This can lead to measurements that are misleading, where the utility of the service shifts from the ultimate value of a course or treatment to subsidiary features of experience. In such cases, reputation, educational degrees, certificates and audits can play an important role, to help assess quality, and forms of oversight may be needed.

Market or organization?

If there are costs attached to markets, are they always preferable to division of labour within an organization?

There are also transaction costs within an organization, between departments and individuals. But there one can better demand information on competencies, results, conditions, intentions and reliability, in ways that could not be enforced on an outside partner. With hierarchical power one can impose resolutions of conflict. One can see to it that specific investments do not lead to one-sided dependence and extortion. Between independent parties that is more difficult: that requires negotiation, in give and take without an overarching boss.

The price one pays for the loss of market by organization within a firm is the loss of its advantages: the incentive for effort to survive, lower price through competition, and flexibility of switching to other suppliers/customers and novel combinations of products and technologies. There is another problem with the integration of disparate activities within an organization. Efficient production and organization require a certain focus of knowledge, mission, goals and ways of dealing with each other in the firm, so that not all things need to be defined, discussed and settled at every step of the way, but can be taken for granted as they are. In other words, a firm requires a certain 'focus' (Nooteboom, 2009).

Earlier the concept was discussed of 'cognitive distance'. Within an organization that should not be too large, for the sake of productive efficiency. That means that if for the success of the firm other activities need to be included, one must seek them outside the firm, in collaboration with others (Nooteboom, 2009). This is a fundamental point that indicates that markets and organization, competition and collaboration are not clear substitutes but complement each other. To achieve efficiency in order to compete, one must collaborate with others to get what one needs but is not able to produce efficiently oneself.

There are intermediate forms. Within firms one can create 'internal markets', by making departments as independent and autonomous as possible, with their own responsibility for survival, up to also having outside partners (customers, suppliers). However, there are limits to this in how far it then still makes sense to include them in the same firm, with sufficient focus. One can also opt for collaboration between formally independent parties, in alliances, in combining competition and collaboration, but for that one must learn to deal with the dependencies involved.

It is complex to weigh these alternatives, but there is a rule of thumb, as follows. Integrate when it is about similar activities, with similar technology in similar markets, and in all other cases go for alliances. The arguments for integration are as follows:

- With the same activities there are more economies of scale, difficult to achieve without integration. Think of the size of a chemical plant.
- Then also cognitive distance is smaller, with equal technology and *modus operandi*, which enhances efficiency.
- Integration within an organization then is easier, with fewer differences in culture (ways of thinking, working, communicating, priorities and conflict resolution).
- With equal products in equal markets the potential conflict of competition is greatest, and the need to control them is greatest, and the opportunity for that is greatest under integration.

In all other cases, so the rule of thumb goes, an alliance is better, because it:

- yields more cognitive distance, with its advantages,
- yields fewer integration problems,
- is more flexible in the configuration of activities,
- can be more gradual than integration by merger or acquisition, and one can step out along the way more easily when things do not go well.

The most important conclusion here is that next to competition collaboration must play an important role in a new programme for economics. That is elaborated on in Chapter 5.

Preaching and practice

In theory, business is a proponent of markets, because that is the current lore and ideology, but practice deviates from the preaching. In fact, one does one's utmost to limit competition where one can, to increase profit. That is the great hypocrisy. The pressure for this comes from shareholders, and personal ambitions concerning the renown and careers of managers.

As indicated earlier, the golden grasp is specialization, in unique products. That reduces direct price competition, yielding higher profit margins, because different products are not direct competitors. Another golden grasp is innovation: coming up with something new that is not there yet, and for which a market does not yet exist. This is fine, it contributes to prosperity but it is not the ideal of perfect competition that leads the ideology of markets.

A legitimate strategy is to temporarily protect an innovation against competition, with patents. That is a deliberate policy of governments, to give innovators an opportunity to recoup the expense and risk of innovation before the market kicks in. If everything could be instantly copied there would be no incentive for innovation.

A less acceptable strategy is to block entry to a market. Upcoming competitors, often small, with

an innovation, are bought up, to freeze or delay
the innovation and to prolong the life of existing
products and investments. Obstacles are raised
to innovation by the complexity of rules, regulations and technical standards, under the pretext of
safety, to slow down innovation. The latter ploy
has been used to slow down innovation in clothing, apparel, toys, furniture, medical equipment,
etc. Switching to a competing product may be
complicated, such as the hassle of the change of
account number in switching to a different bank.
With all this, limiting competition is not the exception but the rule.

At the same time, next to competition, constructive collaboration, not collusion is important in
limiting competition. It is not always easy to
draw the line. I know cases where in order to collaborate in innovation specific investments were
needed, and to recoup such investments agreements were needed for exclusiveness, barring
similar activities with others for some time. The
competition authority blocked that with the argument that such exclusiveness limited competition.
This triggered debate on how constraints could
be adjusted to allow for innovative collaboration
with specific investments.

Concerning constructive collaboration also,
practice does not widely accord with the preaching I have done here. Some firms practise it,
but most do not. There is too much integration,
in mergers and acquisitions, where collaboration
in alliances would have been better. That arises

from weakness: the incapacity to operate other than under the hierarchy of a central authority. According to economic logic, such inefficiency should not be viable under the pressure of markets. But it remains. How can that be?

One factor is the overestimation of economies of scale from integration in a larger firm. In the treatment of those economies it was indicated that there are limits to them, and that there are also negative effects. Often only the advantages are paraded, and the disadvantages are hidden or not seen. The real reasons for the excess of mergers and acquisitions (MAs) are the following:

- CEOs want more power and influence, and MAs help to achieve that.
- Imitating each other: everyone does it, so it must be good.
- If you do not go along you lose out: if you do not take over you will be taken over.
- You have to be first not to be taken over.
- Banks, having an interest in selling their service, oversell it.
- An MA is more spectacular, as a deed done in one go, than the bit by bit crafting of an alliance.

If, then, it is not in the interest of the firm, why do members of supervisory boards allow it? Because they are mostly also CEOs of other firms, and allow the game that they themselves also play.

Power

Economists often shy away from discussions of power, since it is not supposed to exist under market discipline. However, when markets are imperfect economists do speak of 'market power', of a monopoly, for example. But issues of power are more pervasive and fundamental.

What is power? Here I employ a customary definition of power as influence on the choices of others. That can be positive, in offering new options for choice, and freedom of choice between them – with a new product, or a job, for example. Negative power constrains options or forces the choice between them. Negative power typically exploits dependence. That can be the result of monopoly: there are no alternatives for a given supplier. The government tries to prevent that with a competition authority. There can also be power of the buyer, in 'monopsony': there are no alternatives for a given buyer. That also is a matter for public scrutiny.

There can be disequilibrium of power in collaboration. That is important given my claim that there should be more alliances instead of mergers and acquisitions. How can one control risks of dependence in collaboration? That is a subject for the last chapter of this book, on how a new economy would work.

Firm size matters for power, in the opportunity for ruinous price competition, the internal subsidy of one product by another, lobbies and the resources for lengthy legal procedures protracted by expensive lawyers. One can also exert power in a more positive way, in offering unique quality. A monopoly, in other words. So, a monopoly can be used to protect against dependence, by creating counter-dependence.

Power pushes itself on. It is not only addictive, but power evokes counter-power, which in response evokes a further increase of power. The vulnerability of dependence calls for trust, but trust requires trustworthiness. Why would people, organizations or systems be trustworthy? This is a big subject and will be treated only briefly in the last chapter.

A recent development that raises important issues concerning markets is the emergence of the so-called 'platform'. To help producers find and acquire customers, more and more use is made of individual customer profiles to tailor products and advertising to them. The data for it are collected by internet firms such as Facebook, Google and Amazon. They make profit from that. The consumer has mostly given permission, implicitly or explicitly, aware or not, but does not have insight into what happens to the information, how it is combined, packaged and sold.

With some products, such as the taxi service Uber and B&B service Airbnb, the reputations of providers are measured, and are presented to users as a help in selecting providers. That seems useful to the user, and he/she does not seem to care what happens with the data, e.g. those on reputation.

This can yield a serious impairment of legal rights of privacy and fairness. Under the motto of providing transparency of supply and demand lies an opaque, surreptitious profit machine. This is also accompanied by a strong concentration in large firms with monopoly power (Apple, Google, Amazon, Uber, Facebook, Twitter, etc.). There, the underlying effect of scale is as follows. Profit is made from supplying consumer profiles to firms for their advertising, and the quality, diversity, extent and depth of the profiles increases with the number of consumers involved and the spread across activities monitored. How could this concentration occur while in other industries it is prevented by competition laws? Because data do not fall under that law. One of the actions on the agenda, then, is to bring data under that law. Then excessive concentration by mergers/acquisitions can be stopped.

Moral boundaries of markets

Next to the imperfect functioning of markets there is an issue of their moral boundaries. There is a growing literature on those boundaries. A well-known author in this area is Michael Sandel (2012). He gave many examples, including the degradation of value. Something loses its value when left to the market. An example is a prize, such as the Nobel Prize: what is the worth of it when it can be bought and sold to the highest bidder? What is the worth of a diploma when it can be bought?

Sandel also gives examples of problems of justice, such as the following. The mayor of New York wanted to treat the population to a free concert in Central Park. Because of limited capacity and security considerations one did have to stand in line to collect a ticket. A smart entrepreneur collected some vagrants to stand in line for a pittance, to collect tickets which he then sold to the highest bidder. Thus something set up outside the market was snatched away by it.

Now if in some case one is against the market, one should come up with an alternative form for allocating scarce resources. That can be a lottery, a queue, rationing and 'attribution': allocation according to some criteria. An example of that is attribution on the basis of excellence, as with the Nobel Prize. Another is attribution on the basis of need or urgency, as in the 'triage' at hospitals. Forms can also be combined: with equal urgency a queue.

The queue was used in the case of the concert in the park. Lottery applies to a unique product, rationing to a limited supply. The argument for the market would be: let prices rise, to attract new supply. That is problematic when supply is 'inelastic': there are hard limits to supply. Temporary scarcity can lead to extortion, as with the sale of water to the highest bidder during extreme drought.

There are also cases one can debate. What if the rich are offered to shoot a few rhinos at some outrageous fee, to collect funds to protect rhinos

(Sandel, 2012, p. 79)? It is a pragmatic move, given the state of ethics, but perhaps also a betrayal of the ethical principle you want to uphold, of not killing for entertainment.

A well-known case is that of blood donation. In some countries it is conducted as a social gift, but in some it is paid with a fee, and there the quality of donated blood declined because now it yielded income for the poor and the less healthy. Another well-known case is that of the timely pick-up of children from day-care. That happened first as a matter of solidarity with the staff: late pick-up was not done. Then a sum was imposed on late pick-up, and it increased: now one had the feeling that late pick-up was a service one paid for. The market replaced solidarity.

And child labour? An immoral market, one would say. But what if without it people starve? Perhaps one should first address that issue, get children to go to school, and then forbid child labour?

Diversity of markets

Whether and how markets work depends on a number of features. It depends on market structure, with the following features: the degree of 'horizontal' integration, i.e. the integration of competing firms, and the degree of 'vertical' integration of firms that serve as each other's buyers and suppliers. Horizontal integration in particular can limit competition, with agreements ('collusion') on mutual adjustment in price setting and division of the market. That is also the main focus of competition authorities.

Limits to competition also depend on the types of customers – consumers or firms – and their ability to judge the quality of products. It also depends on the degree to which products are bundled, technically or commercially, in distribution or service. It depends on the homogeneity or differentiation of products. Of importance also is the degree and speed of innovation and ease of copying, the internationalization of production, consumption and distribution and, not least, the pollution that occurs and measures to counter it.

Large effects of scale can lead to concentration in a small number of large firms. That can threaten competition, but not necessarily, since it is not about actual competition but the threat of it, with new entrants and the degree to which they can be discouraged by closing off markets with the threat of ruinous price competition with entrants, from reserves that the firms have built up with high profits.

There are more issues concerning the limitation of competition. How easy it is to copy a product, how accessible are the resources required? How high and of what type are the transaction costs? What are the arguments for a merger or acquisition or rather an alliance, and to what extent do they occur?

The next chapter is about how these factors work out, for a few industries, to illustrate the differences. This serves to show that markets are imperfect, in different ways in different industries, do not work automatically, and are not merely a matter of taking out government action ('laissez faire'), but require differentiated measures to reduce imperfections.

4. Industries

This chapter gives a piece of what is known as 'industrial economics' or 'industrial organization'.[1] It concerns the 'meso level', between micro and macro, of industries and markets, where the causality of action really takes place, needed for insight into the 'real economy', with the possibilities and limits of markets and issues for regulation, tailored to the specific conditions of industries.

Earlier, I proposed that the operation of markets depends on the specific characteristics of industries, in the organization of production, distribution, trade, competition and collaboration. I discuss industries in terms of the process in which value is added, in the 'value chain'. It would go too far to discuss all industries: here I discuss a few contrasting cases to illustrate their variety, and consequent differences in the need and form of intervention. This serves as an antidote to the oversimplification concerning markets that is often exhibited.

Such oversimplification was apparent, for example, in the development of the internal market in the EU. It was announced as a matter of 'negative integration': the simple elimination of national regulations, after which markets would automatically lead to simplicity and welfare. The truth was that every industry required its own regulation, whereby on the level of the EU complexity increased, leading to it acquiring the reputation of being a bureaucratic busybody, while on the national level complexity decreased after it was hived off to the EU, which reinforced nostalgia for the supposedly more simple home country, although that rested on a misconception.

Kinds of activity

Of old there is agriculture, growing natural products. Then came the manufacturing industry, in physical production. Next, an increasing variety of services emerged, which now embraces most of employment. The activities produce widely diverging kinds of 'products'. Here, I follow the custom of calling everything a product that yields added value, defined as the difference between sales and purchases, be it a value of form, function, wellbeing, location, information, security, or time. For the retail trade, for example, utility is a value of assortment (range of products on offer), location, service and time (of opening).

Next to commercial services there are public or semi-public services (transport, education, care, energy and water, communication, etc.), which over the past years have increasingly been relegated, wholly or partly, to the private sector, in deregulation or privatization. The question is whether that has gone too far, and how one should now proceed. Thus there is, for example, a discussion on market forces in health care.

The following industries are discussed here: manufacturing, building, agriculture and extraction, personal services, with special attention to health care, and finance and insurance, with special attention to the financial crisis since 2008.

The key characteristics of interest for the operation of markets are the following:

- Scale effects and concentration
- Entry barriers
- Degree of horizontal and vertical integration
- Type of customer: consumer, professional buyer
- Degree to which quality can be judged by users
- Homogeneity vs. differentiation of products
- Technical and commercial (in)separability of products, e.g. of hardware and software, purchase and service, etc.
- Complexity and knowledge intensity of technology
- Patenting of technology
- Degree of innovation: incremental or radical, in product and process.

In particular, together these factors determine the type and degree of competition.

The value chain consists of the stream of incoming things (materials, goods, people, instruments, etc.), processes of transformation (of materials, forms, functions, mental or physical states of people), and then output (delivery, installation, service, maintenance, aftercare). That stream has a direction of flow and is therefore depicted in the form of an arrow. However, in manufacturing there is also the matter of a reverse stream, backwards from refuse and dumping, for the sake of recycling.

Treatment of these industries can only be schematic, with the main points for illustration.

Manufacturing

The key characteristic of manufacturing is the physical transformation of materials and assembly of components, in the formation of some function (see Figure 4.1). It yields a utility of form and use. The type of process determines any economies of scale, important for effects on the increase of scale and concentration. There are different kinds of economy of scale. One is the 'engineering economy' of the volume of processing, in process industries such as oil, chemicals and other material

Stream of materials and goods		
purchase	*Functions* production	marketing
incoming materials, components, machinery	*Activities* physical transformation assembly	sales, distribution service
	recycling	

Figure 4.1   Value chain manufacturing

processing, in reactor vats. Piece production, as in the making of tools, machinery, electronics, and the like, used to be handwork, mostly in speciality unit or batch production, and in comparison with process industries was small scale. That has changed radically with automation, digitalization and robotization. Those now enable mass production of unique products, in flexible production on individual specification. One can now order a custom-made car with its own features, colour, upholstery, engine, etc.

Concerning economy of scale, as discussed earlier, in process industries, as in chemicals, the mathematical law applies that for a spherical reactor the proceeds of sales are proportional to the content (proportional to the third power of the radius) and costs (of materials, cleaning, heat loss) are proportional to the surface (proportional to the square of the radius), so that the ratio of proceeds to costs is proportional to the radius. That law also applies, to a greater or lesser extent, in building and transport, for the size of the construction or vehicle.

Next, there are economies of specialization in the division of labour achieved at higher volumes (Adam Smith's classic example was a pin factory). Often, the ability of users to judge the quality of an industrial product is reasonable, as a 'search product', which enhances competition. In manufacturing there are many forms of pollution, in exhausts (CO_2, soot, sludge, water used for cooling), waste and goods dumped after use, which urgently require measures, such as a CO_2 tax and recycling.

There are opportunities for collaboration, in the pharmaceutical industry for example, between flexible, small, risk-taking ventures for the development of diagnostics, processes and active substances, and large firms that do the testing for regulatory approval, large-scale production and distribution, and marketing under a brand name.

Building

In the industry of building homes, offices, bridges, roads etc., the primary process is one of bringing together at a certain location workers, materials, components and equipment (see Figure 4.2). It yields a utility of form and of location. Most building activity takes place on location, but increasingly modules are fitted together that were produced in a central manufacturing facility.

Architect John Habraken showed that there is a discrepancy between the building of the 'carrier', the basic structure that also contains stairs, lifts and ducts, and the 'infill' of individual homes or

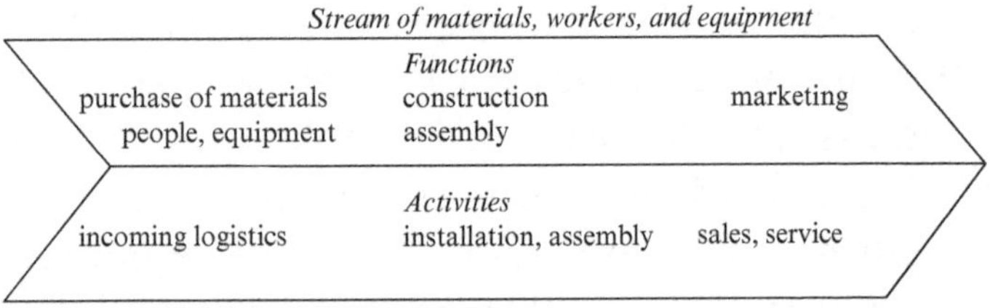

Figure 4.2   Value chain building industry

offices that are 'hung' on the carrier. The first has a long life, of 50 to 100 years, the second a life of 10 to 20 years. In the first, involvement of users is barely necessary, in the second it is desirable, for individual design of the location of walls and fixtures, and materials. It can be compared with roads and cars. To build the two things together is as if road builders should also build the cars. Tailor-made modules seem expensive, but with standardization of measures and components, automation and computing it becomes economically feasible in design where the prospective user is involved, with appropriate software, behind a computer screen.

A building is largely a search product; its quality can be judged beforehand, perhaps with some help from an estate agent. This makes for considerable intensity of competition. There are, however, power differences between developers, builders and buyers. There are important effects of scale, of two kinds. One kind is the economizing effect of large structures, with low circumference relative to usable space. A second kind lies in specialization, efficient use of machinery, and in logistics, in the supply and removal of materials, people and equipment.

The characteristic for building is that it is conducted in projects, not continuous production in one location. As a result, collaboration is intermittent. That can yield complications concerning the 'specific investments' in relations, which require sufficient continuity of the relation. In connection with that, special attention is needed for relations between buyers and suppliers in the building industry. Is that purely transaction-oriented, on the basis of the lowest price, as used to be the practice, or is it oriented more towards collaboration on quality and innovation, with some continuity of the relation? This is part of a wider discussion on the importance and modes of collaboration in the economy, next to competition. That will be returned to in Chapter 5.

Agriculture and extraction of raw materials

As in manufacturing, in agriculture there is the transformation of physical goods, but here it is a process of natural growth, supported with artificial aids (see Figure 4.3). As in building, the process is bound to location and takes place outside, except in cultivation under glass, where it is subject to influence by the weather. The utility offered is one of consumption.

In agriculture there is hire/purchase of land and machines, seeds and cattle, and chemicals, activities of sowing or insemination, maintenance

	Stream of goods	
	Functions	
tilling land	seeding, growth harvesting	selection, transport, marketing
	Activities	
incoming goods equipment, machines	working the land, extraction, harvesting planting, feeding, care, milking	distribution

Figure 4.3   Value chain agriculture and extraction

and care, spraying water and chemicals, harvesting, and distribution and transport to the food industry and the slaughterhouse.

The food industry belongs to manufacturing, with large effects of scale in the production process, specialization, brand name, marketing and distribution. That exerts a large pressure of buying power on agriculture, which creates pressures there towards increases of scale and industrialization of land use and agricultural processes, with the use of machinery for ploughing, seeding, spraying and harvesting, and automation, e.g. of milking. This often occurs in cooperatives, for countervailing power to the food industry, which often nevertheless wind up being dominated by it.

This dynamic has led to an increase of scale and concentration in land use, with a proliferation of homogenized land, with damage to varieties of landscapes and the habitat of flowers, birds and insects, due also to spraying against diseases, and an excess of manure, herding animals in cramped spaces, with risks of contagion and low quality of animal life. Measures are urgently needed to redress this in a different kind of smaller scale, more environmentally friendly, circular form of agriculture.

The quality of agricultural produce can mostly be judged fairly well by consumers, except for the content of toxic and other health damaging materials, for which tight regulation of production, sales and marketing is needed, under control by a health authority. Products are highly subject to differentiation, in processing, content, taste, additives, salami tactics and packaging, which limits the efficiency of competition.

The extraction of raw materials, such as oil, coal, aluminium, salt, stones, diamonds, uranium, and a variety of other minerals, e.g. for electronic devices, is similar to agriculture, and to building, in being location-bound. It is less sensitive to weather and season, with exceptions such as oil drilling in high seas, and projects are of longer duration.

Composition and quality can be well judged by professional buyers. Raw goods are the typical case or fairly homogeneous mass products, with limited differentiation. Therefore, raw materials form the paragon example of close to perfect markets. However, scale effects arise in specialist expertise, as in seismic exploration, bulk transport of the materials, transportation and use of machinery and installations, and the spread of risk of 'dry wells'. As a result, extraction industries are large scale and concentrated and exert excessive power, particularly in in the often underdeveloped countries where the raw materials are found. Extraction yields pollution of land and air, in extraction itself and next in separation and purification, and transportation of the materials.

Both agriculture and extraction are the subjects of scientific research, biology, chemistry, geology and process technology, investigating soil, ground water, irrigation, animals, plants, fertilizers, husbandry, climate, etc. In the Netherlands there is a separate university for agriculture. All this makes it clear that these industries are necessarily subject to extensive monitoring and regulation.

Personal services

A key characteristic of services is that the product is largely immaterial ('you cannot drop it on your toes') and that production and consumption mostly occur simultaneously and at the same place, with a customer undergoing treatment. Here I focus on personal services (see Figure 4.4) and not, for example, on knowledge services such as education, training, consultancy, etc. There is a wide spectrum, in many forms of personal care, housing, sports, entertainment, communication, media, transport and hospitality industry (cafes, restaurants, hotels). I will discuss medical care separately, in view of discussions concerning the introduction of markets in that field.

In all cases the primary process is one of 'processing' people, in some form of treatment of mind or body, with requisite equipment and materials.

These services give a utility of bodily or mental

	Stream of customers	
	Functions	
arrival, placement	servicing	departure

	Activities	
reservation, booking,	treatment, care, entertainment,	payment,
incoming goods,	catering, accommodation,	departure,
people, parking	registration	aftercare

Figure 4.4   Value chain of personal services

wellbeing, and to some extent of security and reliability. Largely, it applies here that consumption and production go together in time and place, but there is often a 'back office' for activities without customers such as preparation, administration, training, storage and research.

Products are mostly experience goods, whose quality is determined during consumption, and judgement in advance requires reviews and customer reports. There are few switching costs from one supplier to another, even though providers try to engage in binding customers with special customer cards, discounts, etc. As a result, competition is quite intense. An exception is health care, where it is difficult for the customers (patients) to judge the quality of treatment. There are also distinctive effects of scale in specialization and the purchase and use of expensive instruments and installations (such as an MRI scanner). That is why it will be treated separately.

Scale effects arise especially in brand name, which is why there are often chains of facilities, or a franchise chain under the umbrella of its name, for restaurants, hotels, health shops, hairdressers, etc. For independents there are often cooperatives to achieve volume discounts in purchasing.

Health care

Health care is an important case of a problematic effort to let markets work in public service. Here the discussion is mostly of hospitals. That is a complex issue, with no room to be complete.

Such care used to be a public task, on the basis of a budget system, but over the last ten years a transformation has taken place to make it work more like a market. Here I will focus on the case of the Netherlands. Typical for health services is the split between producers (hospitals), customers (patients) and those who pay (in the Netherlands: the insurance companies). The basic problem is that patients cannot properly judge the quality of medical treatment ('cure'), which is a credence good. Care by nursing is largely an experience product, whose quality can be experienced during the process. This separation between producer, user and payment raises fundamental problems for the operation of a market. The ruse that was invented was to let the one who pays, the insurer, conduct the judgement of quality, and competition between insurers would guarantee that they would be motivated to do it well. Alas, the insurer cannot judge quality either.

The central goal of making care work as a market was to reduce costs, which threatened to explode due to the aging of the population and an explosion of technological possibilities in medicine.

To make judgement by insurers possible, in 2005 care was categorized in 30,000 types of treatment, called 'diagnosis–treatment combinations' (DBCs). Since 2013 they have been called DOTs ('DBCs on the way to transparency'). A problem with that was that it raised transaction costs enormously, while the goal was saving expense. A second, more fundamental problem is that, as is well known in the literature on 'communities of practice', professional work cannot well be captured in such codified protocols. It can work for simple, standardized treatments, such as that of a broken leg, but not in other cases of more complex cures. A third problem is that innovation requires experimentation and the protocols should not be so strict as to lock that out. Also, if medical practice is thus locked up in protocols, it weakens the own responsibility of doctors: they can hive off responsibility onto the protocols, and a generation later doctors will not be up to meeting their own responsibilities.

Where formerly there was room in a given treatment to do something more or different where that seemed necessary, now a second DBC must be 'opened', even if that goes too far and is not quite needed, which increases rather than decreases the volume and cost of treatment. I give the example of my daughter. She had to undergo a root canal treatment on a molar. During the procedure the dentist found that the neighbouring molar also needed treatment. It would have been logical to include that, in an extended treatment, but that was not allowed, and a new DBC had to be opened for it, for which my daughter had to return, again with a prescription from her GP.

The system also encourages fraud from unnecessary claims or even claims for unperformed treatments. A newspaper of 27 September 2018 reported that in 2017 there was a 27 million euro fraud. The insurance companies now look critically at the statements of expense, but in the judgement of unnecessary claims doctors can claim doctor–client confidentiality.

How about freedom of choice for the 'consumers'? One can go only to the hospitals accredited by one's insurer. And then there is the following paradox. The fundamental merit of markets is that they give room for individual freedom of choice and initiative, but here in the name of markets the freedom of choice of patients and doctors is curtailed. That happened for the sake of improving the comparability of treatments. Freedom was curtailed to improve comparability.

Is there an alternative? One is a periodic professional peer review, as is practised in the Netherlands. That could also have been used in a state health system.

Another fundamental issue is that while the costs of health care can easily be measured, quality cannot be. Thus, the focus is on costs, not quality. In 2016 I heard a director of an insurance company say that they 'had not yet come around to quality', and that was ten years after the introduction of the new system.

There is a profit motive to offer expensive 'nonsense care', which is difficult to judge, with an appeal to fears of health hazards, or vanity, especially for the rich, with unnecessary tests and investigations, and treatment for minor ailments of weakness, indigestion, unease, overweight, etc.

Insurance companies are tempted to engage in premium differentiation on the basis of 'risk selection', with higher premiums for higher risks, e.g. of obesity. Often the poor have a less healthy lifestyle, and they would be hit most. Such differentiation thus had to be forbidden, at least for basic care.

There has been an increase of mergers between hospitals. As elsewhere, in other industries, those occur with shaky arguments. As argued elsewhere in this book, arguments are adduced of economy of scale, but the disadvantages are neglected. I give an illustration. Some years ago, I was called in to adjudicate in a clash of views concerning a merger between what was considered to be a 'core' or 'top-clinical' hospital, oriented towards complex, difficult to plan, intensive care, with specialized facilities and staff, and another type of hospital called a 'satellite' or 'categorial' hospital with simpler, run of the mill, plannable care. The second resisted the merger, in order to retain their motivation in developing and maintaining their own competencies, e.g. in coordination with the 'first line' care by GPs. After some debate, the crux of the issue appeared: the simpler care was more profitable, and the core hospital wanted to benefit from that to cover its costs and risks. The problem thus lay in the fact that the remuneration of complex care was not in line with its costs, and instead of finding a solution for that the solution was sought in an ineffective merger.

The pressure now exists to extend the market

to letting hospitals act as independent firms with limited liability and shareholders to whom dividends could be allocated. The argument is that with that hospitals gain access to capital that they do not have now. That is not nonsense, but there are reservations. It is predictable that, as happened to building societies, investment will follow profit opportunities even if those lie outside the goals of hospitals. With the building societies those were luxury holiday resorts for rich pensioners instead of affordable housing for lower middle classes.

More profit also entails more risk, and this can lead to the same problems as with banks: a hospital can then become 'too big to fail' or 'too sensitive to fail' because default would entail loss of care, leaving patients uncared for, so that the risk is hived off onto society, in bailing out the hospital. It also makes hospitals vulnerable to *hedge funds*, private investors who work outside capital markets, buy up firms, impose a high debt to finance it, and a fee for themselves, and pay that off by creaming off revenues with lower wages, redundancies, economizing on investment and R&D, and hiving off less profitable activities, which increases short-term profitability, after which the firm is brought back onto the market with much profit.

All in all, when we look forward, in anticipation of an accumulation of adverse effects, the question is whether we are on the right track. In conclusion, I can only see this development in health care as costly and counterproductive. Can it be turned around or mended?

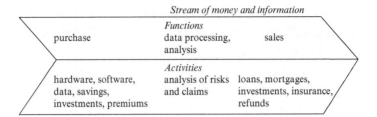

Figure 4.5   Value chain finance and insurance

Finance and insurance

Finally, there are services in finance and insurance. The value chains of these activities are sufficiently similar to be put together in a single scheme, illustrated in Figure 4.5. Finance and insurance are connected in that proceeds from insurance premiums are invested for profits, and financial risks may in turn be insured. This similarity and connection explains why finance and insurance have increasingly been integrated in financial corporations. By combining them costs can be shared, e.g. of retail outlets, specialization, knowledge and information, spreading risks, reputation and brand name, which are subject to economies of scale.

This industry is similar to knowledge industries, where the analysis of data, here about financial markets, revenues and risks, is a core activity. In finance a science has developed concerning asset pricing and the valuation of options. In insurance there is a science concerning 'adverse selection' (how people with the worst risks have the greatest interest in insurance) and 'moral hazard' (how once insured people become careless). These analyses share an underlying quantitative science of probabilities and statistics. The complexity of analysis in maths and statistics has increased, whereby they are not always well understood, even within the industry.

In the value chain, there is an incoming flow of funds from saving accounts and insurance premiums. At the incoming side of the chain there is search for customers, with development and sale of a portfolio of products for saving and insurance. Incoming funds from savings and insurance premiums are invested in an outgoing stream of loans, and insurance claims processing yields an outgoing stream of refunds. Here there is marketing, at the outgoing side of the chain, in the development and sale of loans, mortgages etc. There is an important reverse flow of information from markets, concerning revenues and risks and related customer conduct, to feed the input of data for improved assessment of revenues and risks.

Finance and insurance both yield utility of funds, diversification of risk, and assurance. To some extent these services have characteristics of an experience good, in the support and the speed of service experienced. Consider, for example, the speed of claims processing in insurance. However, they are also to a large extent *credence products*. It is difficult for most customers to assess whether correct advice and implementation is given. A large part of utility is security against financial default. This is so large that a central bank is required to monitor bank practices. For remaining uncertainties reputation and brand name are of great importance.

There is also *moral hazard* in the combination of finance and insurance. There is a temptation to run high risks in finance, and sell them, and gain extra revenue by insuring them.

The distribution of products, in particular mortgages, for a large part went through intermediaries, e.g. estate agents. That yielded the perverse incentive that for remuneration they received a share in the revenue, which jeopardized their independence and objectivity with regard to financiers and insurers. This has led, in the Netherlands, to the correction that now their services are paid for by the consumer, which increases the intermediaries' independence and their incentive to cater to the consumer's interest, and increases the competition among them.

In the share market instability is built in. If shares are valued at market value, and the market is in a dip and the value of shares declines, that increases the burden of debt, which is now covered less, so that more cover must be found by selling shares, which further depresses their value. In good times the reverse happens. Normally, with rising prices demand will fall, but here the reverse happens: the rise of share value is taken as a signal to jump on the wagon and buy more shares, which further pumps up their value, which causes a bubble, with an increasing debt covered by the higher value of shares, until the bubble bursts.

In view of the crises since 2008 there is much to say about this industry. In part, that is done elsewhere in this book, but here follows an elaboration, to contribute to the explanation in terms of perverse financial products.

A bubble arises with 'futures'. Those entail that one commits to sell shares at a future date at current prices. One loses when prices rise but saves when they decline. Thus, they are a hedge against decline. But increased sales of futures is a signal of loss of confidence in shares, an expectation of decline, which causes further sales of futures, going on until the bubble bursts, futures become worthless, and in response share prices fall.

What also contributed to the crisis was that opaque packages of slices of risky property (such as dubious mortgages) were sold to customers who could not judge the risk. In that way, banks shed their risks while making a profit out of it. By the sale, risks disappeared from the balance sheet, by which banks had less bother from demands of minimal reserves, so they could continue to play their game of excessive risks. When customers catch on that they cannot judge risks, they rely on credit rating agencies, but those are not reliable. They were paid by the banks whose riskiness they had to assess.

Another perverse product is that of the CDS: credit default swap. With that, A as a provider of credit to B can insure the risk at a third party C. That can yield an incentive to A to contribute to the default of B, in order to cash the benefit from C. C has an interest in a fall in the confidence in B, so as to raise the demand for CDSs. When B defaults, C has to pay the benefit, but acquires the assets of B at a bottom price, and if that was underestimated by the actions of C, C can make a profit on them. CDSs were also traded, so that speculation on them was encouraged. They enable banks to shed risks and free capital that would otherwise have to be kept as collateral. The buyers did not have such obligation and thus risk dropped out of sight.

CDSs were used to gamble as insurance against the financial failure of countries (e.g. Greece). In case of failure one cashes the insurance. Then it becomes in the interest of the issuer to stimulate that failure. That could be done by extending excessive loans, and earning an additional profit on that, and to have the creditworthiness of the country overestimated, if necessary by helping the country to hide the risks with bookkeeping tricks. The CDS has been compared to a fire insurance that I take out on your house, after which I set your house on fire.

An interesting intellectual failure of banks lay in the calculation of probabilities in the judgement of risk. They assumed probabilities to be independent (as in a 'random walk'), where a high chance here is compensated by a low chance there. But in a crisis they all go in the same direction, e.g. in prices of houses or shares, in bubbles and their burst. Central banks did not catch on to all this until it was too late. And then there was a lack of intervention when insight cleared. But central banks are faced with a dilemma. On the one hand they have a task to oversee banks, which pleads for intervention, but on the other hand they have the task of ensuring financial stability, which argues against sharp intervention. Intervention at a bank would publicly demonstrate the problem, with the risk that this would cause a general loss of confidence in banks, yielding a cascade of failures, resulting in a system collapse. The Ministry of Finance should have intervened but it was too close to the banks.

Conclusion

The foremost conclusion of this chapter is that markets are not simple, certainly not as simple as market advocates make out. They vary greatly between industries, with a corresponding variety of problems, with needs and possibilities to avoid or redress them.

Candidates for efficient markets are undifferentiated mass products, easy to judge on quality, no switching costs, no scale effects and no entry barriers. Those do not exist. Mass products, such as primary goods, tend to exhibit effects of scale.

Gasoline, for example, appears to qualify as a homogeneous mass product, but oil companies manage to turn it into speciality, by means of brand names, logos, colours, shops at gasoline stations with special offers, and loyalty cards. Also, they have one-sided power over operators of stations, exert one of the most powerful political lobbies, pressuring for tax facilities, and lenient or delayed environmental policies.

The case of hospitals shows how difficult markets can be in public services.

The case of financial markets shows to what extremes markets can derail in the private sector. I once thought nothing could be so homogeneous and perspicacious as monetary assets such as funds and shares, but ways were found to make them opaque, obfuscating risks or hiving them off onto society. Exchange rates, in particular, seemed to qualify (what is more homogeneous than money?), but it turns out that they have routinely been manipulated.

My conclusion is not that markets should be abolished but that they should be systematically understood and monitored, sometimes with extended regulation, taking into account the differences between industries.

I now turn to the last chapter, to give theoretical and practical details of a new economics to deal with these and other problems.

5. A new economics

This chapter begins with a comparison of the main points of old (mainstream) economics and the new economics proposed here. Then there are some concrete policy proposals. Subsequently a detailed discussion is given of the basic 'logics' and principles.

A new programme

Earlier in this book, mainstream economics was represented as a 'research programme', as proposed by Imre Lakatos, with a 'hard core' of basic assumptions and principles. Here I present a programme that is virtually its opposite: An 'economics of the other'. The differences are summarized in Table 5.1.

The points in the table are elaborated on in the following paragraphs.

I do not claim that the old (mainstream) economics is wrong everywhere and always. It still applies, approximately, under the following conditions: the values ('utilities') involved can be measured, preferences and choice options are known in advance, with their possible outcomes ('pay-offs'), for oneself and the others with whom one is engaged ('pay-off matrix'). Then one can calculate

Table 5.1   Old and new

Old (neoclassical)	New (economics of the other)
Rationality	Limited rationality, heuristics
Autonomous individual	Socially constituted individual
Optimal outcomes	Processes of adaptation
Efficiency	Development
Competition	Competition and collaboration
Risk	Uncertainty
Utility ethics	Virtue ethics
Instrumental value	Instrumental and intrinsic value

an optimum, or an equilibrium (in game theory), and it would be silly not to take that opportunity. When, on the other hand, one or more of these conditions are not satisfied, under uncertainty and when preferences, options and outcomes are emergent rather than pre-established, then the step to the new economics is needed.

I illustrate this with a formative experience I had when employed by Shell Oil, in the 1970s, as a project leader in the computing centre at Shell Centre in London. There, we used optimization techniques for the scheduling of refineries, the routing of ships, location of gas stations, design of loading stations for natural gas, risk spreading in portfolios, etc. For strategic planning, by contrast, uncertainty was too large to allow for such techniques of optimization, and we developed scenario analysis of possible futures, with simulation for analysis of the robustness of alternative policies across different scenarios as more important than optimality.

Political economy

The context here is that of political economy. In the first chapter of this book, in a discussion on liberalism, I sketched the development of the economic thought of Keynesianism until the end of the 1960s, until the development of neoliberalism, from the 1980s. It was a development from fiscal policy in government expenditure and taxes, aimed at maintaining employment, to monetary policy, aimed at the control of spending and inflation. From attention to government and the demand side to attention to firms in markets, on the supply side.

What now? The Keynesian thesis that government should spend during slumps, at the expense of a government deficit, and save during growth, for a decline of debt, still seems like an elementary truth to me. However, my attention does go to firms, on the supply side, but then in a balance of interests of capital, labour and society: markets, but only where they are desirable and then with corrections of their imperfections; international trade, but with constraint of its excesses, with maintenance of local communities and the prevention of a 'march to the bottom' in social conditions, employment and taxation under the threat of multinationals to outplace employment.

There should be less obsession with finance, more attention to the real economy, knowledge, development and production, and measures to orient shareholders to the longer term. I cite Stephanie Mudge (2018, p. 367): 'Market society should no longer be an alternative to human existence but a means to it'.

More concretely: policy measures

Before I continue with theoretical foundations, how does all this work out in more concrete policies? Here is a non-exhaustive survey.

Nationally

- Different composition of supervisory boards of businesses – representatives of shareholders but also of other stakeholders: employees, customers, suppliers and local communities (for the sake of the environment).
- Next to competition, for standardized goods, also collaboration, in specialities and innovation.
- Fewer mergers and acquisitions, and more alliances, adjustment of competition policy to allow for this.
- More 'horizontal control', next to taxes and health care also in education, building, municipalities, etc.
- More local democracy and local communities: citizens' councils, elected mayors and municipal council, entrepreneurial communities sharing resources and spreading risks in joint projects.

- Car/road tax as a function of car use, according to volume and time.
- Subsidy of public media and press (to stop the race to the bottom of quality of literature).
- No further markets in care.
- Circular agriculture.

EU

- Transformation of financial markets to a longer-term perspective, if needed, with protection against takeovers, e.g. by hedge funds.
- Uncoupling of retail and investment banking.
- Restriction of bonuses and of difference in remuneration between public and private sectors.
- General CO_2 tax.
- Further control of tax evasion.
- Let data fall under competition policy, to prevent excessive concentration of platform businesses in information and communication, such as Facebook, Google, Amazon, etc.

Cultural/mental

Furtherance, in education, of:
- The classical virtues of reasonability, courage, moderation, and justice.
- Appreciation of diversity, tolerance.
- Ability to cooperate, trust, and 'cross cognitive distance'.

- Resilience to uncertainty and setbacks, adaptiveness.

More in detail, concerning banks: split banks into banks for spending and saving accounts, and investment banks. The first fall under government guarantees, the second do not. As long as that does not happen:

- Stronger restrictions on 'leverage', the ratio between debt and reserves, higher reserves.
- More transparency of subsidiary firms and side activities that do not fall under central bank scrutiny.
- A minimum of mortgages to be kept on the balance sheet.
- No more bail-out.
- Limit bonuses and stock options and install *claw-back* of them when speculation goes wrong.
- Impose a standard measurement of risky investments.
- For calculating the interest rate for tax on property and for pensions, use not the actual rate but a trend value.

These proposals are not new, but I would add:

- Limit the practices of hedge funds.
- Limit speculation with credit default swaps.
- Value assets not at the present market value but at a more stable trend value.

- Let risk management take into account system risk, using data also from periods of instability.

Some proposals entail a limitation of markets, others an extension of them.

Public choice

I plead for more regulation of market imperfections, but I acknowledge that regulation also has its imperfections. There is a literature on that, on 'public choice'. The most important problem recognized there is that government is not subject to the discipline of competition in markets, so that there is room for too many inefficient rules, with inefficient execution. That is debatable. There has been political pressure towards limited government expenditure and austerity. And the argument works two ways. Without market pressure there is also less incentive to profit at the expense of citizens.

A second point of criticism against 'public choice' of politicians and civil servants is that they are not purely determined by considerations of public benefit but also by political expedience and opportunism, with an eye to elections and coalition formation. There is myopia towards the next elections. But in financial markets the view is on the next quarterly results.

A third point is that the political carousel of rivalry, negotiation and tugs of war regularly issue in unintended effects, desired by none. And one should take into account the (im)possibilities of implementing tangled compromise.

A fourth point is that politicians and civil servants are not always driven by an ethic of public service but rather by a personal interest in position or career, in profiling themselves with new regulation. But that also cuts both ways. It can also lead to the neglect of regulation under pressure of lobbies by interest groups and the personal interests of politicians and civil servants in positioning themselves for future careers in business or other interests. Vigilance is needed on both sides: against both over- and underregulation.

How new?

The policy measures listed for the 'new economy' are not new: one finds them in the media. What, then, is new here? That lies in the argumentation for them, from the perspective of a new economic and philosophical framework, and argumentation is crucial for debate on policy. The proposals are based on the foregoing chapters, and are delved from insights and methods from economics, sociology, social psychology, cognitive science and philosophy.

A new argumentation is needed because the present situation is one of hypocrisy and hide and seek. The liberal ideology of markets has stumbled along in failure, and has become a charade. Firms profess it but try to increase profits in the widespread obstruction of competition and pressure on governments to grant financial and regulatory advantages under threat of moving their activities abroad when not accommodated.

Politicians play hide and seek in holding market ideology high while often markets are not in fact realized. Examples are a CO_2 tax that would yield a market mechanism against pollution, fair tax practices, tax on car use according to volume and time of usage, which would yield a market mechanism against congestion. At the same time, markets are introduced where they are undesirable (education, science, culture) or are problematic in their functioning (care).

According to liberal ideology ethics is not a public matter while in fact it is inevitable in public discourse, and then is conducted surreptitiously, as an add-on rather than basis for policy. The right to exist for firms is to satisfy demand in society. The most pressing demand now is to save the environment, but most firms circumvent that.

The flag of liberal ideology has long failed to cover the actual load of what in fact is no more than a pragmatic, compromised, muddling through without an ethical compass. It is time to provide underlying arguments that fit what actually happens and face the imperfections of markets.

I claim that this cannot work on the basis of the utility ethic that underlies market ideology; it requires a virtue ethic with the classical virtues of prudence, courage, moderation and justice that in fact already impose themselves on public debate. These are: reasonability towards populist complaints; the courage not to tag along in system tragedies; moderation of greed and remuneration; and justice in the distribution of income and access to knowledge, legal process and political voice, and in the conditions and continuity of work.

While the ideological lore is that of utility ethics, apparently that does not stand up in the light of experience, and in fact debate is conducted in terms of the virtues mentioned, but this must apparently be hidden or masked. Who nowadays is honestly arguing for greed, purely personal interest, maintenance of increasing inequality of property, and erosion of solidarity, education, care and culture?

A plea for virtue ethics is often ridiculed as naive, but here I merely make explicit what has played out for a long time in human experience, but was then unclear and confused. I also claim that it makes not only social but also economic sense.

What difference would it make? Socially and environmentally responsible entrepreneurship, more stakeholders in supervisory boards of business, more continuity of labour and relations, a long-term perspective on investment – those would no longer be compromises with market ideology, but would form the core of what society and the economy are about. Not justification of society to the market but vice versa. Not without markets but with proper use of them.

How this thinking works out is discussed below.

Exit and voice

Albert Hirschman (1970) made the distinction between *exit, voice* and *loyalty*. In exit one walks away from a relationship, fires people and sells part of a firm, when dissatisfied. In voice, one expresses discontent, asks for deliberation, with the intent and commitment to come to an agreement, to solve problems together, with pooled resources. In loyalty one has no choice or no desire for exit or voice and one submits to the inevitable.

An authoritarian regime, in business or government, tries not to give room for either exit or voice – no exit in voting for another leader, no voice in freedom of expression. It can then happen that one convinces oneself that authoritarian dictatorship is in fact what one wants or needs; that its powers are in fact beneficial, with good intent, because it would be psychologically intolerable to face the arbitrariness of the terror. That happened, for example, under Stalin. Little father Stalin must have his good reasons.

The old economics is directed at exit: markets are about competition, choice, substitution; one or the other. To offer something is 'take it or leave it', not deliberation about how something could or should be. Developing countries complain about how aid is given in this way, without a say from themselves. And aid is then dominated by neoliberal myopia.

In the new economics, the default is not exit but voice: try that first and go for exit only when that fails. This is aimed at collaboration, complementarity and profiting from difference. That applies also to markets. It is better, for the user as well as the producer, for the user to voice complaints and for the producer to listen, in order to improve his product. Keeping a customer is also cheaper than winning a new one.

Exit is oriented towards the short term and voice to the long term, with investment in the future of a relationship. As argued by William Davis (2019), the exit mode has damaged society more widely than only in markets, with people grasping it whenever not satisfied. Firms and citizens exit in tax evasion, in the threat to move activities elsewhere when they do not get their way. Populism also appeals to exit: away from the EU, from parliamentary democracy, from 'the elite'.

Now, public services have been 'sold' as 'products' for the citizen as 'customer', and marketing has taught that 'customer is king' and 'the customer is always right'. It is understandable, then, that government as supplier must always give the citizen as customer whatever it demands. Davis claims that this also lies behind Brexit: the familiarity and dominance of exit. That cannot work in a democracy, because there the crux is voice, in compromises, not a dictate, not exit.

Trust is the art of voice – openness about what you are unhappy with, giving the other the opportunity to explain and improve. I will expand a bit on trust later.

Rationality and heuristics

How could one still maintain that people make rational choices? In economics bounded rationality has long been taken into account, but only in a limited sense. The argument was the economic argument that capacity for rational thought is limited and hence must be spent according to priority (e.g. by Herbert Simon). A distinction was made between substantive and procedural rationality. Concerning procedure it is rational not to judge everything substantively. Therefore conduct is largely based on routines, in which people act without conscious reflection. That argument makes sense and is still valid. Without routines life would not be viable. Imagine that in driving a car one would need to think about it. Then one would not be able to pay attention to where one is going, or to conversation with a fellow passenger.

But there is more to it, as included in recent 'behavioural economics', which employs insights from social psychology. That concerns so-called decision heuristics that are procedurally rational but not substantively. Here is a survey. The heuristic of 'availability' is that one pays attention to what is 'available', i.e. strongly presents itself to consciousness, in emotion, often as a threat or an opportunity. That can go wrong, in neglect of less emotionally loaded but still important things, but it helps in setting priorities for awareness. It does, however, contribute to impulsiveness, prematurity and emotionality, which are already rife in present society. The danger of routines is that one sticks to them when they no longer apply, as in an impending car accident. You then need the shock of emotion to catapult you out of the routine to take appropriate action. So, while availability may not always be rational, it has the value of adaptiveness.

Another heuristic is that a perspective of loss ('loss frame') carries more weight than a perspective of gain ('gain frame'). One goes to greater extremes to prevent loss of something than to gain it if one did not already have it. While not always rational, that also has its rationale. Loss can lead to hurt or death, and thus the priority of loss probably arose in evolution. It also has a stabilizing effect on relationships: the one who wants to exit wants that in order to gain, the other stands to lose and may go to extremes to prevent it. Loss, seen as a threat, may trigger aggression in the amygdala, the centre of such emotions in the brain.

A third heuristic is that of 'representativeness'; incidents are raised to laws: 'You always with your . . .', while the . . . only happened twice or so. That is unreasonable but can have survival value, for timely response to threat.

A fourth heuristic is 'escalation of commitment': to the extent that in a given situation one has incurred loss, it gets more difficult to get out, because then 'the losses would be in vain'. That is not rational. In the choice between staying or getting out one should look only at future gain and loss, because there is nothing one can do about the past. That is water under the bridge. This also works in favour of continuing a failing relationship, often against better judgement. It can also be positive, in an entrepreneur tenaciously holding on to his project, in spite of setbacks, which especially in innovation inevitably come along. A classic case is that George Bush found it hard to get out of Iraq, because then 'all the deaths of soldiers would have been in vain', a politically sensitive issue. It would also amount to an admission that the decision to enter was wrong. To get out, a new president was required, Obama, untainted by the wrong decision (and he went on to make a similar mistake in going deeper into Afghanistan).

A fifth heuristic is that one limits oneself to only incremental adjustments while the initial position was widely off the mark, and a radical switch is required. Thus, one can keep muddling with a relationship that was misguided to begin with. This also makes for continuity of relationships.

A sixth phenomenon is 'cognitive dissonance', where after a choice one has attention only for information that justifies the choice. In continuing a difficult to break relationship one only wants to hear good things about the partner, and after a break only the bad things. That is understandable. One is confronted in life with hosts of contradictions or oppositions that are difficult to reconcile: present and future, self and other, reason and emotion, body and mind, excitement and calm, truth and lies, and one does not want to have to admit after each choice that it may have been the wrong one.

A seventh is 'adaptive expectations'. One strives after what one wants but is not content when having it, and wanting, expecting more. One works oneself into stress and then is not satisfied with the outcome. The poor are envious of the rich and the rich are not content with what they have.

'Nudging' is on the rise. That recognizes these non-rational choice mechanisms and tries to correct them or turn them around for choices that are better for those involved or for society. There is much to say about it, but I will not do so here. Here the point is that it recognizes and utilizes the pervasiveness and impact of the imperfectly or non-rational heuristics.

Individual and social

The human being is not autonomous, is still an individual but is socially formed, on the basis of interaction with others and a shared culture. Culture here is primarily anthropological: habits and customs, and morality, on the basis of more or less shared ethics. While that is shared, what is made of it is individual, along one's own life path. That yields diversity, and that is bothersome but also productive. See the earlier treatment of 'cognitive distance'.

Earlier, it was indicated that for its development the human being requires recognition and interaction, in local communities with a certain stability, but also some circulation and external contacts. That can be done in two ways. One is more decentralization of governance to municipalities or city quarters, with an elected mayor and citizen councils, with or without political parties. The problems and possibilities of this were discussed earlier.

A second possibility is a halt to further flexibilization of labour, with more continuity of work and teams. That is good for the quality of labour and for the quality of products, which require specific investments that need some continuity to recoup.

For this, and for innovation, the environment and a just future for the young, a long-term perspective is needed, no longer the obsession with next quarter's profits. If shareholders cannot muster that perspective then they should no longer have a majority, in a supervisory board that also seats representatives of labour, consumers and the local community, for protection of the environment. Economists will comment that this would raise the price of capital, but if that is what it takes, so be it.

From optimal to adaptive

The customary assumption of rational choice with optimal outcomes, in old economics, yields an excuse not to look at the processes of what actually happens, and whether those do or do not realize the optimum. That yields a neglect of reality, with the complexity and differences between industries discussed before.

It is necessary, for both public policy and management, to act on the basis of insight in those. There is a myth afoot that for management it does not matter where one is a manager, since management is the same everywhere. On the contrary, one must have knowledge of and insight into the fields of force inside and outside the firm, in the terms discussed earlier: customers, suppliers, technologies, economies of scale, entry barriers, degree to which products can be judged, transaction costs, protection or sharing of knowledge, integration, alliances, etc.

On the macro level it is meaningful to see the economy and industries as evolutionary systems of variation, selection and transmission of success. Government intervention can then be addressed, as much as possible, to the conditions for that, rather than direct intervention in conduct.

Competition and collaboration

In markets, relations of supply and demand serve mutual interest, until there is one-sided power or dependence. Competition authorities have the task to oversee that. Next to instrumental, material interest, of the price and quality of the product, relations, including market relations, can have intrinsic value, in the quality of dealing with each other, and considerations of moderation and justice arise. Are people goaded on to excessive consumption? How are the labour conditions in making the product? In the warehouses of Amazon is minimal delivery time so important that the stressful labour conditions are warranted?

Between producers there can be both competition and collaboration. When is the one good and when the other? That depends: good for whom? For society, competition is good when it indeed yields efficiency and low prices, and is not socially or morally undesirable. For the one who loses the competition of course it is bad, and therefore there is an incentive to limit the competition. Between competitors there is a zero-sum game: the one wins what the other loses. One can also look at it in another way: losing is instructive. For some, there is delight in competition – the challenge to win, but also delight in harming the victims. The difference lies in fair play and justice.

When, then, to select not competition but collaboration? That is not so difficult. Competition has its place when conditions for it are best satisfied: it concerns existing supply and demand, limited scale effects, limited transaction costs, including ease of judging quality, in relation to sale and purchase, no specific investments, and no switching costs.

Collaboration is more in order when supply and demand are still under development, quality or innovation requires a combination of different competencies and other sources, and those entail specific investments that require some duration of the relationship. Here there is a positive-sum game, with advantage to both sides.

This does not mean absence of rivalry or tension. It entails mutual dependence and that requires ability in dealing with that: the issue of governance, the management of relations of dependence without a hierarchical 'boss'. That is difficult for many, because one is not accustomed to it, in mentality, thought and action, and lacks the requisite knowledge and competence for it. But those can be learned.

There are instruments of governance, such as contracts, material incentives and reputation. One can also aim for sources that go beyond pure material self-interest, in ethics, morality, empathy, friendship, or identification. The latter go beyond old economics, and therefore I elaborate on them.

If collaboration entails more or less mutual dependence, with the risk that it is manipulated to gain a greater share in jointly created value, how does one deal with that? When is it right to try and manage that with contracts and other forms of control, and when to allow more room for trust? The latter can be risky but is cheaper, and next to instrumental value, can yield intrinsic value to the relationship.

Purchase and supply

Here the discussion goes more deeply into relations between purchase and supply in business.[1]

Traditionally the game was all about price. The buyer specified the demanded product, suppliers did their bids, and the one with the lowest price

won. That works fine for stable, standard products, but not for specialized, specific or innovative
products. Then it is odd to seek suppliers that can
do things you cannot, and yet pretend to be able to
tell them what to do and how. It makes more sense
to involve them in the design and development of
one's product, to make the best contribution to
the end product. The supplier can then show, for
example, how in leaving out bells and whistles
one can lower the price, or, to the contrary, how
one can add more value. That often requires
the specific investments discussed before, which
require a certain continuity of the relation to
recoup them. This *modus operandi* is accompanied
by *open-book contracting*, where buyer and supplier
share resources in a joint endeavour to achieve the
highest quality at the lowest price. Then, the supplier cannot keep his/her costs and order portfolio secret for the sake of price negotiation. To
offer such openness he/she requires a guaranteed
profit margin above his/her costs. The buyer then
sets the maximum price he/she is willing to pay,
deducts the profit for the supplier, in *price minus
costing*, and that yields the envisaged costs of production for the supplier, in a joint effort to achieve
it, in a pooling of knowledge and competence.

For the sake of recouping the specific investments involved, the supplier is guaranteed a
minimum duration or volume, but after that the
choice for the buyer lies open again. That leaves
an incentive for the supplier to do his/her best,
because if he/she performs well, he/she is the

first in line for the next round. In the car industry, for example, the duration could equal that of the lifetime of the present car model.

This practice was first conducted in the Japanese car industry, and was subsequently adopted in the West, but not entirely. The openness in sharing knowledge in Japan raised the fear of *spillover*: the leaking of knowledge via the supplier to competing car producers. Against that risk, exclusiveness was demanded from the supplier, where the supplier was not allowed to supply to a competing car producer. That yielded vertical *keiretsu*: pyramids with the buyer at the top, and first-tier suppliers locked up in supply to that buyer only.

That had a negative effect: the supplier was locked up and curtailed in its potential to learn from practices elsewhere. That is also not to the advantage of the buyer who imposes the restriction. That demand for exclusiveness was not adopted by the Western car industry, on the basis of the following insight. If developments go so fast that competing car producers do not have the time to effectively utilize the spillover, then the problem disappears. Next, the Japanese, in turn, copied that, and this led to the dismantling of the *keiretsu*.

Governments, nationally and in the EU, have imposed regulation concerning government procurement; that it must be public, and open to foreign suppliers, and that one is pressured to accept the bid with the lowest price. That goes against the logic set out here. As argued above, the specific investments require a certain continuity of custom, but that implies a temporary limit to competition, and that is against competition policy. This requires an adjustment of that policy to allow for the new logic.

Power and dependence

Dependence yields power. I employ the definition of power as having influence on the choice of others. That can be positive, in widening choice options, or negative, in limiting them and imposing a choice from the available options. With negative power, one may wind up in a vicious circle of mutual constraint. There lies the danger of an excess of oversight and control, out of fear of risk of dependence. There are alternative modes of operation.

What are the sources of dependence? One is monopoly: the partner offers something no-one else can. Another is switching costs: exit is expensive, you are locked in. Now there is a paradox. Specific investments make you dependent, but when they are used to offer specialities, in collaboration to offer something unique together, that can yield countervailing power in becoming a monopolist yourself. Your partner cannot do without you, and therefore cannot afford to exploit you. Here one arrives at a virtuous circle: both sides do their best to offer something so unique that the other cannot do without.

Another stratagem, when specific investments

become one-sided, is to demand that its ownership and cost are shared, to balance the risk.
Countervailing power can also lie in the ownership of other sources, or access to them, that the
other needs, such as the use of a patent, access to
a market, or lobby to a government, or a coalition
with third parties.

As noted, another relational risk is that of spillover: the unintended leakage of sensitive information. That can be direct, with the threat of the
partner becoming a competitor, or indirect, in the
risk that information leaks via the partner to a
competitor of yours that he/she also has a relation
with. That was discussed above, in the discussion of relations between purchase and supply.
The risk of spillover is often overestimated. The
question is not only whether sensitive information reaches a competitor, but also whether he/
she is able to absorb it, and has the possibility, in
personnel and means, to actually transform that
into effective competition. If by the time that has
been achieved the information is out of date, the
problem disappears.

An important feature is reputation. Partners
restrain themselves not to spoil opportunities in
future relationships. For that there must be a
reliable reputation mechanism, where gossip is
separated from legitimate complaint.

One can also use hostages. A hostage is something of value to the hostage giver but not to the
hostage taker, so that the latter will not hesitate to kill
the hostage when the hostage giver reneges on his

commitments. To give an illustration, years ago, the then minister of economic affairs in the Netherlands was interviewed on television concerning his involvement in a joint venture between the Japanese car manufacturer Mitsubishi and the Swedish manufacturer Volvo, for the production of cars in the Netherlands. The stake for government was to preserve high value employment, in design, development and production, at the company itself and at its suppliers, and to prevent the factory shrinking into a mere 'screwdriver' factory for the assembly of components produced elsewhere. Yes, the interviewer said, but how can you be sure that the Japanese will stick to their commitment? Well, the minister said, at home I have a shoe box containing the designs of the new model, and those are the property of the Dutch government. So what? the interviewer asked. Well, the minister said, if they do not honour the agreement, I can sell the designs to a competitor – Ford for example. This also illustrates that in time the hostage can die a natural death. The car from the designs has now long ago appeared on the road.

Beyond control with countervailing power, or reward, punishment, reputation and hostages, one can seek a way in trust, on the basis of values, ethics, morality, empathy, identification, friendship and routinization. Below, I go somewhat deeper into trust.

In view of all the complications of collaborative arrangements it is tempting to avoid them and place relations under hierarchical control, in a merger or acquisition. But that is a cop-out with its own problems, and has the disadvantage of less diversity in the relationship, due to the need to integrate, less flexibility in making novel combinations, less focus on what one is strong in, and fewer incentives for the survival of departments that are assured of their internal custom. The challenge is to resist this reflex and learn the art of collaboration between independent partners.

Trust

Trust is a big and complex subject, and here its treatment can only be summary. For a more extensive treatment, I refer to previous work (Nooteboom, 2002).

It is unchallenged, also among economists, that in a general sense trust is indispensable: without trust there could be no money. It is the task of a central bank to uphold that trust. And one needs trust in other institutions, such as property rights. And the failure of a bank must not be allowed to escalate into a loss of trust. Banks exploit that by hiving off risks to society, forcing it to bail them out. Maintenance of trust in the currency yields untrustworthiness of banks.

However, economists do not accept trust between market parties. Here I refer to several times, around the turn of the century, that I debated this with Oliver Williamson, Nobel Prize winner and one of the fathers of the theory of transaction costs. His thesis had two parts, as follows. First, and I agree with this: if trust does not go beyond calculative self-interest it does not add anything. Enlightened self-interest, defined as the willingness to give something away provided that one can be assured to recoup it later, has long been part of economic rationality.

Williamson's second thesis was that trust cannot go beyond self-interest, in giving something away without expectation of a reasonable return. That would be the definition of altruism, and one cannot afford that under the pressures of competition in markets, because then one would not survive. Trust, he argued, is to be reserved for family and friends, outside the economy. I claim the opposite: without trust one cannot survive in the economy. Under uncertainty, where one does not know what can happen, one cannot calculate whether there will be an adequate future return for present sacrifice. One needs trust, in a leap of faith across the gap of uncertainty. There lies the main importance of the virtue of courage.

There is a deeper, philosophical need to take the interests of others to heart, to open up to them.[2] One needs opposition from the other to grow, intellectually and spiritually, in trying to escape from one's prejudice, as the highest level of freedom. This requires that one should not try to enforce everything by contract or hierarchy. That creates a straitjacket that precludes productive surprise. One must be prepared to accept uncertainty, but this does not mean that one should not try to limit foreseeable risks. Those are primarily risks of dependence, discussed above.

Next to the virtue of courage for the leap of trust, dealing with uncertainty requires the virtues of moderation and justice, to grant partners their success. It also requires resilience, the ability to absorb setbacks, and versatility and creativity, to adapt to unforeseeable conditions. As noted earlier, one cannot predict but one can analyse scenarios to seek out robust policies. Uncertainty can be a torment but also a challenge, a Nietzschean challenge one might say, to act in this way.

Trust entails giving room for action to others, and thereby running risks. One can release control to give more room, or narrow it, with increased control. Trust entails belief in trustworthiness but that has to be earned in trustworthy conduct. It cannot be taken for granted. It is wise to take trust as the default, and narrow the room for conduct and increase control when conduct proves unreliable.

Trust is not being nice. Precisely because there is trust people can be open to each other and demand openness, honesty and exercise voice. Openness is key to trust. It requires that one announces errors as soon as they are detected, and resists the temptation to try and hide them, which is seldom successful. Sooner and later they will come out and then one deserves the complaint that if one had announced it before, the problem might have been redressed or mitigated. Openness also requires the virtue of courage, since in admitting error one makes oneself vulnerable. It also requires that one extend benefit of the doubt, when something appears to go wrong: give the other the opportunity to explain and make amends when needed. That requires reasonability, another of the cardinal virtues. Such openness also helps the other to help you, knowing what you expect and are afraid of. Openness is needed about expectations, to prevent the disenchantment that can trigger suspicion and the collapse of trust.

Horizontal control

Oversight is needed, inside firms, between firms, between government and firms, and in politics. However, that has accumulated into a monstrous behemoth, which now strangles professional work, innovation, the taking of one's own responsibility, and the intrinsic value of work with a degree of autonomy. It has spread across society, in taxation, health care, public benefits, education, housing and public administration.

That does not fit especially in present times where work has become increasingly professional, specialized and knowledge-intensive. One employs people, or works with partners, because they know and can do things one can't and yet one pretends to be able to tell them what to do and how, or what exactly should come out from their performance. It demonstrates distrust and the illusion that all risks can be foreclosed. Again, this neglects the pervasiveness of uncertainty. It flies in the face of a whole literature on 'communities of practice', that shows how professional work cannot be caught in closed protocols because it is too rich, i.e. diverse and context-dependent, variable and subject to change, and also can vary with style of execution.

It is not only that control has increased in extent, spreading over more and more activities, but also that it has changed its form. There is no longer personal, face-to-face contact, to take into account specific, individual conditions. Control has become formalized, in protocols that controllers must employ, and computerized. That is a loss in view of what was said above: professional work cannot be caught in closed protocols, and requires attention to variations of context, style and change.

A different form of oversight is possible, called 'horizontal' control, which gives room for trust and is also cheaper. Some ten years ago I was asked by the Dutch Ministry of Finance, on the basis of a publication of mine, to help in the development and introduction of what came to be known as 'horizontal oversight' in the taxation of firms and the internal accountancy of government. According to my information since then, this has caused great relief in those areas. It works as follows.

Instead of imposing self-invented controls, one asks the object of control how it can best be controlled, and then one negotiates how that might work and can best be implemented. It is a good example of the notion of 'voice', discussed earlier.

Both sides have an interest in this, for three reasons.

First, it is geared to a minimum number of key controls. That is cheaper, faster, and leaves more room for autonomy and the richness of professional work, customized service and innovation.

Second, since the proposals come from the work floor, there is a guarantee that the controls are feasible, effective and more to the point than controls imposed from outside. Agreement on the form of control arises face to face, with regard to context.

A third benefit is that it yields a learning system. The controlling authority learns more and more about what works in practice, and thereby becomes a more attractive partner for discussion, and this favours the dissemination of experience.

With all this, there is a sanction. If someone does not play an honest game and does not honour agreements, there is the penalty of falling back into the old, top-down, detailed, outside form of control. Thus, trustworthiness is rewarded with a lighter, cheaper and more effective form of control.

As in many systems of oversight, there is a risk of 'regulatory capture', where the supervisor is entangled in interests and loyalties towards the object of control. One should consider that, and it helps to rotate supervisors across objects. Such horizontal control of hospitals by health insurance companies started as part of the system of health care introduced ten years ago. A complication there was that if hospital agreements differed between different insurers, things would be confusing and inefficient. Going for alignment between insurers was against the basic idea, in the new system, that insurers should compete, and alignment would go against competition policy. That had to be overcome by the allowance to adopt an agreement made by a competing insurance company. This form of control only concerns the administrative legitimacy of the submission and processing of claims for remuneration by hospitals. Any such oversight of the quality of health care is still far off.

The odd thing now is this. I hear that agreements about horizontal control between insurers and hospitals are next implemented within the hospital in the old vertical control. One should also implement horizontal control within the hospital. Let staff come with proposals as to how the agreements with insurers can best be implemented on the work floor.

Something similar might apply in the building industry. In the Netherlands there are also plans to introduce the working of a market, with independent, private, mutually competing controllers. However, for efficiency and the prevention of too much complexity, the controllers must employ a collective pool of instruments, under government supervision. One may innovate, with new instruments, but must then contribute that to the collective pool. That is twisted: where is the incentive to innovate if you must share with competitors? This regulative mongrel is another illustration of the twists taken in the craze towards marketization everywhere.

Currently I am involved in a discussion of the potential of horizontal control in the oversight of courts of law.

Political positioning

To what political positioning does all this lead? I sympathize with some of what lies behind the populist revolt: derailed neoliberal market ideology, with excessive globalization, increasing inequality of property, deterioration of the quality and security of labour, decline of public services, tax evasion by corporations, dishonesty of banks, and power play in lobbying by business interests. I am in favour of more direct democracy, on the local level of municipalities or city quarters, discussed earlier. I am more sceptical concerning national referenda. I am radically against renewed nationalism, authoritarian leaders, suppression of multiculturalism, discrimination of Muslims, and the warding off of refugees. I am in favour of the EU, as indispensable for international cooperation on environmental protection, refugees, defence, foreign policy, financial policy, but under the condition of shifting to a less neoliberal, more social society, with social wellbeing, and social and economic justice.

I think this might yield a renewed perspective for the left. Attention to the intrinsic value of relationships and the need for local roots connects with an old inspiration from Christian traditions. To liberals I say that liberal democracy should be upheld, but the libertarian view of markets is to be rejected, and that the individual should be seen as socially constituted, with local roots, oriented towards other people and civility, as a person, not just an individual. That social constitution does not oppose individuality but enables it, while maintaining unique individuality, everyone along his/her own path of life. And finally: morality and ethics are not only for behind the front door, but form an indispensable part of public life and debate.

Conclusion

To conclude, I return to what perhaps is the most important, or at least the most fundamental issue. To achieve the stated goals, and intrinsically for society as a whole, a shift is needed from the now dominant utility ethic to a virtue ethic, with the classical 'cardinal' virtues of reason, courage, moderation and justice. Reason is needed for reasonability: offering arguments and listening to them, and that requires toleration. This does not mean that there should be no emotion. In the discussion of decision heuristics it was shown that in decision making emotions are needed to set priorities, get attention and to escape from routines when needed. Also, emotions have intrinsic value.

Courage is needed to live with inevitable uncertainty, the impossibility to predict, especially in relations. It is needed to trust, to be resilient to set-backs, to fall and stand up, and to be trustworthy oneself. And to stand up for the virtues.

Moderation is needed for a brake on greed and lust for power. Self-interest is legitimate but should not determine all. There is nothing wrong with pleasure if that does not derail in greed and insatiability. Moderation is needed in remuneration and bonuses, and in a bridle on lust for power. The legitimate urge to manifest oneself in making achievements can express itself without achievement being measured in wealth.

Connected to those virtues is the virtue of justice. Trust, justice and reasonability require empathy, and the ability and willingness to cross cognitive distance. That also benefits one's own development.

One aspect of reasonability is that if one objects to a system, one should come up with an alternative, and if possible an elaboration of it. I have tried to do that in this book.

Notes

Chapter 1

1. For a treatise on the evolutionary roots of morality, see Ridley (1996).
2. A classic text criticizing the dislocation dynamic of capitalism is Karl Polanyi's *Great Transformation* (1944).
3. I am building here on a stream of philosophy of 'Embodied cognition'. See, for example: Lakoff and Johnson (1999), Damasio (2010).
4. See the website iffrome.org.uk, and for further cases, indie-town.uk
5. An international group of leading financiers and academics.

Chapter 2

1. A key, pioneering source of evolutionary economics is Nelson and Winter (1982).
2. With n people the number of possible direct links is $n(n-1)/2$.
3. A key text on this is Kahneman and Tversky (2000).
4. I think Sidney Winter was the first, in his doctoral dissertation.
5. The distinction between negative and positive

freedom goes back to Isaiah Berlin (2017) and was developed by Amartya Sen into the idea of 'competencies' to achieve goals.

6. Nooteboom (2012). There, I try to find a way between Nietzsche and Levinas.
7. The model was tested econometrically in Nooteboom et al. (2007).

Chapter 3

1. Here I make use of an earlier book of mine: Nooteboom (2000).

Chapter 4

1. I taught that for years, in 1980–1990, at the business faculty at the University of Groningen. Here I make use of earlier work: Nooteboom (2014).

Chapter 5

1. Here I tap from earlier work: Nooteboom (1999, 2014).
2. Here I make use of Nooteboom (2012).

Bibliography

Armstrong, Karen, 2006, *The Great Transformation*, London: Doubleday.

Berlin, Isaiah, 2017, 'Two concepts of liberty', *Liberty Reader*, New York: Taylor & Francis.

Cassidy, John, 2009, *How Markets Fail*, London: Allen Lane/Penguin.

Damasio, Antonio, 2010, *Self Comes to Mind: Constructing the Conscious Brain*, London: Vintage.

Davis, William, 2019, 'Leave and Leave Again', *London Review of Books*, volume 41, pp.9–10.

Fukuyama, Francis, 2018, *Identity: Contemporary Identity Politics and the Struggle for Recognition*, London: Profile Books.

Hayek, Friedrich von, 1937, 'Economics and Knowledge', *Economica*, volume 4(13), pp.33–54.

Hirschman, Albert O., 1970, *Exit, Voice and Loyalty: Responses to Decline in Firms, Organisations and States*, Cambridge, MA: Harvard University Press.

Kahneman, Daniel and Amos Tversky (eds), 2000, *Choices, Values and Frames*, Cambridge: Cambridge University Press.

Kay, John, 2003, *The Truth About Markets*, London: Allen Lane/Penguin.

Lakatos, Imre, 1978, 'The methodology of scientific research programmes', in J. Worrall and G. Curry (eds), *Philosophical Papers*, volumes 1 and 2, Cambridge: Cambridge University Press.

Lakoff, Gary and Mark Johnson, 1999, *Philosophy in the Flesh*, New York: Basic Books.

Mudge, Stephanie, 2018, *Leftism Reinvented: Western Parties from Socialism to Neoliberalism*, Cambridge, MA: Harvard University Press.

Nelson, R. Richard and Sidney G. Winter, 1982, *An Evolutionary Theory of Economic Change*, Cambridge, MA: Harvard University Press.

Njeri Kinyanjui, Mary, 2019, *African Markets and the Utu-Ubuntu Business Model*, Cape Town: African Minds.

Nooteboom, Bart, 1999, *Inter-firm Alliances; Analysis and Design*, London: Routledge.

Nooteboom, Bart, 2000, *Learning and Innovation in Organizations and Economies*, Oxford: Oxford University Press.

Nooteboom, Bart, 2002, *Trust: Forms, Foundations, Functions, Failures and Figures*, Cheltenham UK: Edward Elgar.

Nooteboom, Bart, 2009, *A Cognitive Theory of the Firm*, Cheltenham, UK and Northampton, MA, USA: Edward Elgar Publishing.

Nooteboom, Bart, 2012, *Beyond Humanism: The Flourishing of Life, Self and Other*, London: Palgrave-MacMillan.

Nooteboom, Bart, 2014, *How Markets Work and Fail, and What to Make of Them*, Cheltenham, UK and Northampton, MA, USA: Edward Elgar Publishing.

Nooteboom, Bart, Wim P.M. van Haverbeke, Geert M. Duijsters, Victor A. Gilsing and Ad v.d. Oord, 2007, 'Optimal cognitive distance and absorptive capacity', *Research Policy*, 36(7), pp. 1016–1034.

Polanyi, Karl, 1944, *The Great Transformation: The Political and Economic Origins of Our Time*, Boston: Beacon.

Ridley, Matt, 1996, *The Origins of Virtue*, London: Penguin.

Sandel, Michael, 2012, *What Money Can't Buy*, London: Allen Lane/Penguin.

Sapolsky, Robert, 2019, 'Biological perspectives on inter-group conflict', in Muli Wa Kyendo (ed,), *Fundamental Theories of Ethnic Conflict*, Nairobi: The Syokimau Cultural Centre, p. 35.

Skidelsky, Robert and Edward Skidelsky, 2012, *How Much is Enough?; Money and the Good Life*, London: Allen Lane/Penguin.

Skidelsky, Robert, 2009, *Keynes; The Return of the Master*, London: Allen Lane/Penguin.

Stiglitz, Joseph, 2002, *Globalization and Its Discontents*, London: Norton.

Williamson, Oliver E., 1993, 'Calculativeness, trust, and economic organization', *Journal of Law and Economics*, 36(1), pp. 453–486.

WRR, 2019, *Geld en schuld: De publieke rol van banken* (Money and debt: the public role of banks), The Hague: WRR.

Index